Sarah - I am now 'The Dish' so you
can Eat Me! Lol! Lisa-Joseph

Pre-children, Penny Isaacs was a city
solicitor and is now a freelance
marketing consultant to her old firm. As
a freelance legal journalist she has
contributed legal-based news-led pieces
to the *Independent* and *The Times* on
high profile events. Penny is married to a businessman and
they live with their two young children in North London.

Sarah Lockett is a TV news reporter and
anchor with many years' experience
covering major news stories in the UK
and internationally. She has worked for
the BBC, Sky News, ITN, Channel Four
News, Reuters etc. She is currently
working as a freelance TV presenter/ reporter and
combining motherhood with writing.

THE DISH

A 21st century guide to captivating
a Dish, his friends and virtually everyone
else you know using home cooking and a
little homespun psychology

Penny Isaacs
& Sarah Lockett

t₂

Troubador Publishing Ltd
9 De Montfort Mews
Leicester LE1 7FW, UK
Tel: (+44) 116 255 9311 / 9312
Email: books@troubador.co.uk
Web: www.troubador.co.uk/matador

ISBN 978-1848761-018

A Cataloguing-in-Publication (CIP) catalogue record for this book
is available from the British Library.

Cover photograph © Mike Carsley

Typeset in 11pt Sabon by Troubador Publishing Ltd, Leicester, UK
Printed and bound in Great Britain by TJ International Ltd, Padstow, Cornwall

T² is an imprint of Troubador Publishing Ltd

To our husbands, Stephen and Peter.
Per ardua ad astra.

Weave a circle round him thrice,
And close your eyes with holy dread,
For he on honey-dew hath fed
And drunk the milk of Paradise

Kubla Khan
Samuel Taylor Coleridge (1772-1834) English poet

Contents

Introduction: Stepping up to the plate   xi

1.   *Establishing base-camp*
   The ultimate first meal   1

2.   *Consolidating your position*
   Suppers *à deux*   9

3.   *The lone soldier*
   How to deal with the unattached best friend   33

4.   Befriending the WAGS   39

5.   *Being Florence Nightingale*
   Tending to the Invalid   51

6.   *Avoiding confrontation*
   Being the perfect step-mother   59

7.   *Ex-girlfriends and ex-spouses*
   All's fair in love and war   69

8.   *Reaching High Command*
   How to win over the in-laws   77

9.   *An army marches on its stomach*
     Breakfast, brunches and light meals   87

10. *In the field – Al fresco dining*
     Picnics and Barbecues   109

11. *Sports evenings with the lads*   127

12. *Casual suppers with the troops*   133

13. *Power dinner parties*   151

14. *Off-duty drinks parties*   169

15. *Grand gestures and little gems*
     Gifts which hit the target
     and those which miss the mark   179

16. *Triumph*
     Announcing the alliance   187

17. Top tips on how to be CookSmart   191

Preface

It's an old adage that the way to a man's heart is through his stomach. Yes, we know it is the 21st century and, when it comes to eating, the idea of you cooking to impress a dishy bloke is not in your lexicon. You've probably got a tick-list of hot restaurants.

But, come on girls, food IS the zeitgeist. It may sound old-fashioned but being able to nurture/feed/entertain your man and his friends/work colleagues/boss/parents is very attractive. Particularly now when the credit crunch means even banking superstars are crying into their soup. It says marriage material, rather than I-can't-boil-an-egg-I-haven't-even-got-a-pint-of-milk-in-the-fridge brief dalliance material. Your home cooked cuisine (and the type of restaurants you treat a man to) will convey a powerful subliminal message about you. And, dear reader, before you decide to 'recycle' this book by giving it to your spinster cousin, Dorothy, for Xmas, we would like you to know that this is not a cook book, although there are a few killer 'result' recipes included. We are doing something different here – you will be embarking on a unique voyage to help you snare your man using his appreciation of food, be it home cooked, ready made or eaten out. You will learn too about 'CookSmart', our system of maximising flavour while minimising work, AKA a stiletto in an oven glove.

Pour yourself a glass of wine. Better still, bring over the bottle and we'll join you.

Key

Man of Your Dreams (aka The Dish)	MOD
Prospective Mother-in- Law	PML
Prospective Father-in-Law	PFL
Plum Bottler	PB
Wives and girlfriends	WAGS

Introduction

Stepping up to the plate

"Food comes first, then morals"
Berthold Brecht (1898-1956) German poet and
playwright

What's the deal?

Let's start by asking a simple question. Do you recognise this woman?

'Vivacious and attractive female, 33, 5'5", GSOH, educated and in full-time employment, enjoys good food and travel, has (mostly) presentable friends, seeks handsome, sociable, intelligent and unattached male 30-45 for fun and romance, wining and dining and – who knows – possibly a long term commitment.'

This is YOU and we believe that this is the classified ad you would like to - but daren't - place and which, thank goodness, your mother hasn't submitted on your behalf. If we are correct, then read on. If not, please donate this book to one of your mates.

Let's start with some need to know basics about this book. Whilst this is intended to be a thoroughly modern, practical guide to getting yourself singled out by a dish of a man by appealing to his taste buds, this is no ordinary cook book. If you found it in the 'Cooking' section of the bookstore would you mind asking the manager to move it to the Best Sellers, I mean, the 'personal relationship' shelf.

What we shall be doing is learning how to send coded but decipherable messages to this paragon to convey to him that you are his ideal life partner. The key points which you will learn to subtly convey are that you :-

- add value to every facet of his life
- are a competent cook
- are a superb hostess and
- look the part – ie glamorous.

We are assuming that you have found the MAN OF YOUR DREAMS; he's 6ft tall, dark and handsome and lives in a penthouse in Chelsea Harbour or similar fabulous part of town. Actually, it would not matter one iota if he is short, balding, and an accountant from Pinner. The fact is you adore him. But here's the rub. At least until the credit crunch gets him too, he will be working in an office with a bevy of willowy Czech beauties all of whom could be the next supermodel and his svelte Bulgarian PA has just dumped her boyfriend. How do you begin to compete for his affections?

We both know from our own experiences of dating that modern women seeking a long-term partner have a more difficult task than their mothers/grandmothers, particularly if their target is a successful man about town. This gent probably lives on his own or, at least, away from mum and can cater for himself quite nicely. Whether it is ready made meals, takeaways, delicious deli grub from his local traiteur or a fat expense account, he will be eating well. He does not need to be rescued from malnutrition!

Nevertheless, how about setting a culinary honey trap? Let us convince you of the benefits of adopting an intelligent approach to gastronomy to trigger your fellow's matrimonial antennae. Our aim is to get him to project *you* into a future setting as his wife/partner where you will be not so much looking after him as showing him you fit into the life he wants. The key point is to prove yourself as a capable and glamorous hostess, NOT a housekeeper.

Realise now girl, that some foods light up a man's eyes – like chilli, garlic or steak. And other foods leave him cold – like light salads, steamed fish and greens. Cook him the RIGHT foods on your first date, and you'll snare him for life. But serve him the wrong things – girl-food like quiche and soufflés, and you'll send him running. This book tells you what to serve, what atmosphere to create and what not to do/say/wear. Lay the correct bait, and you'll catch your man.

Accordingly, in the chapters that follow, we shall explain how to hone specific skills centring around meals designed to convince your dreamboat that you are special. Ranging beyond what's on his plate we will be using the performance, yes, the theatrics and alchemy of the kitchen and the dining room, to win him over. You will be making an investment here and there by taking him out but, don't worry, this will be covered nicely too.

For the purposes of our thesis what must you do? There are one or two preconditions. First, you need the courage to reappraise *fundamentally* your attitude toward food preparation. Do not see dishes in isolation. Instead, we advocate a rounded approach wherein what you make is in harmony with the setting. You must then achieve a state of spiritual karma. Engage in lots of meditation and *tai chi*, in the lotus position, balancing some bananas on your head. Actually, get real! You will learn that our approach is quite grounded. The second caveat is that you trust us to devise a clever culinary strategy where all meals are going to be carefully choreographed to suit the occasion *and* the audience.

And to spice things up – we think we can do more than just impress your beau. Can you think of people who might be thorns in your side? We can. There will inevitably be an annoying best friend and pulling partner who regards girlfriends as short-term disposable commodities, plus there is bound to be at least one pest of an "ex" bombarding him with texts. They have to go – and we will show you how. This may seem calculating and hard-hearted, but all's fair in love and war. You're just maximising your chances and minimising the ex-girlfriend's/football pals' chances of getting their claws back into him and dragging him away. We shall be employing some deft kitchen moves to see off these unwanted diners.

Be warned. This is not a one-way street with you as a passive participant. We shall be enlisting your whole-hearted co-operation in turning yourself into a versatile actress. Theatrical experience, even from schooldays, will be a definite bonus. Why? To pull this scheme off you are going to have to be a chameleon since we will demand that you cast yourself in different roles for each of the situations you will find yourself in as we progress in this relationship.

A brief glimpse of where you are headed – amongst your Oscar winning performances will be:

(a)   the charming, confident, supportive hostess – easy
(b)   the approachable, child-friendly step-mother – dig out and study some old Lassie films – a new version has been released on DVD recently.
(c)   Florence Nightingale/the school matron for when he is under the weather – think Hattie Jacques in the *Carry On* films.
(d)   homely Anne of Green Gables for the in-laws – surely you read the book?
(e)   a girl with an invented obscure food intolerance for the WAGS – it'll be a laugh.
(f)   a sweet thing for the best friend and his ex – stiletto time.

We will also be citing food-related anecdotes about friends and relations and others who have had walk-on parts in our lives. We would both wish to continue to enjoy their hospitality and goodwill. Speaking as a trained (although admittedly no longer practising) lawyer I can assure you that there are to the best of my knowledge no defamatory remarks in this book, and Sarah and I have no libel cover.

But, since some individuals may be of a shy disposition we have decided against referring to all individuals in this book by their real names. Except for husbands, of course (who I hope are smart enough to realise we meant them if we were to refer to our other halves) we have chosen new identities largely at random, although I confess to have plucked names from some of my favourite TV shows – Alias, 24, Sunset Beach (yes – I was glued to every episode of this last fabulous series and daydreamed about being cast as a new character - Olivia's long lost sister from England).

So, is this strategy ruthless? Excuse me, but we resent you using a description like this. We have clean consciences and so should you. You love this man, he may even love you. It is just that the competition is hot and in his face five times a day. Accordingly, it makes sense to take some pretty radical measures to make him fully appreciate your finer qualities. For this reason we prefer the term 'being professional in one's approach'.

Contrived? We would say organised. Kindly explain to me what is the difference between what we are suggesting and refining your CV, smartening up for an interview or tarting yourself up to go out? The only person who will dislike what you are doing is a love rival sitting at home shaving her legs while you are cooking up a storm. Let's not give the poor girl a second thought.

Ambiance

More than what to eat, we propose to offer blunt advice on how to create a seductive background *mise en scène*. By this we mean the décor, music, table setting (yes, we are serious!) and all the other details that go into an effective evening's entertaining, apart from the food. For a start, your clothes speak volumes. We are going to make no bones about telling you where we think you may be going wrong with your outfits and what you should wear to help mould a sassier, more alluring image. The idea will be to forge a distinctive sense of style, not to be a rigid follower of vacuous transient trends.

Labels will mark you out as high maintenance (quite the wrong message as the country heads for recession) and, in some instances, middle aged. Use them sparingly. This may sound a bit like your mother talking, but there's nothing wrong with that! Take it from a couple of old(er) birds who've been round the track a few times and figured out what works and what doesn't. The formula for bagging a decent chap really hasn't changed that much over the years so follow this advice and you'll get results. Speech over.

And, by the way, since we suspect you are short of strong female role models, we will be nominating someone for you to emulate as an icon at the beginning of each master class. We make no apology for the fact that we have largely drawn these women from screen sirens of the 1950's and 60's. In my (many) idle moments I confess that I fantasise about being one of them, preferably with Carey Grant on my arm. Sarah's much more diplomatic and says she would not want anyone else other than hubby Peter! Ahh.

Incidentally, are you curious to know who my role model is? Please do not think I am a crank but, I believe in some bizarre way, that I could be a long lost descendant of Fanny Fern (1811-1872). It was this formidable writer who made famous the phrase 'The way to a man's heart is through his stomach'.

Whilst we do not share common ancestry I feel that there is a kind of synergy in our attitudes. She had a finger on the female pulse in terms of her understanding of how relationships really work and the angst that accompanies them. Fanny sought to highlight and empathise with women and became an ardent supporter of the suffrage movement. I hope I can equal her insight into the interaction between the sexes in the 21st century.

Fanny Fern was actually the pseudonym of Sara Willis, the first female columnist in America, famous for her conversational, satirical writings. She buried one husband, divorced another and forged a successful career for herself in her 40's after falling on hard times. Fanny was clearly a woman of determination, wicked humour and ability. Ahead of her time, she did not let family ties or the lack of emancipation impede her career. To me therefore she represents a beacon of determination to succeed against the odds.

As for little old me, what is my story? Well, when I last checked, my first and current husband, Stephen, was still alive. I always say I am 31 and you will have to ask my bank manager if I am on my uppers. As for Sarah, she's on her first and last husband (if he plays his cards right, she says). And as we are adjusting our ages here, she's 29 (might as well go the whole hog).

Getting back on track, as well as clothing, music matters too. Since there is going to be some clattering of pans while you bring your creations to life, a little background entertainment will be useful to divert attention from the stove. We will be making pleasing musical selections – so make a list of these. They will be unobtrusive but modish. Not trendy or the latest thrash/house/garage tracks.

Head to PC World. The first thing we shall insist upon is that you demonstrate how up-to-date a girl you are. Abandon the ten year old CD player your dad gave you for your 21st and buy an IPod with attached speakers. This will look cool. You can then either download the right tracks or record them from your CD collection.

Sarah's way more up to date with music than me and has a rather nifty idea about what you could do. She points out that if you are too techno-phobic to master iPods (as in fact we both are) then go with your CDs but put them on repeat, so you don't have to keep dashing off to change the CD, or worse, suddenly notice the glacial, pounding silence in your head that means you've run out of conversation AND music, just at the same moment.

Finally, the old fashioned counsel to a host - to ensure a pleasant evening - was to avoid contentious subjects, notably religion and politics. I can see that we are going to have to update this advice if you are to sidestep embarrassing faux pas. More importantly, you may agree that finding the right thing to say to a dining companion can be more taxing than the food. Never fear, we will be making a few suggestions on how to make conversation flow as well as the wine.

CookSmart

By the time you have done with this self-help manual we hope that you will have become a devotee of the CookSmart approach to cuisine.

Naturally you are intrigued to know what CookSmart is all about. Well, in the main it encapsulates a confident approach to cooking. Follow my pointers and see what it does for you. To join the CookSmart club here are some outline do's and don'ts.

Do's
We would like to see you becoming self-assured enough to do the following:

(i)   You need to pick up a saucepan without flinching. You must be capable of presenting every dish effortlessly and with panache, thus bewitching your beloved into believing that you are marriage material.

(ii)   You should treat cooking as fun, not a chore. Forget about relying too greatly on precision. It is taste that counts. Provided you employ strong flavours and top notch ingredients you will never again fret about slavishly following a recipe.

(iii)   At the end of this book you should not think twice about flirting between ready made and home made dishes – you will of course be buying in some items which you are banned from making – pastry, soups, cakes and quiches.

(iv)   You will use robust fresh ingredients to create maximum impact. Modern food suffers in equal measure from being boring and/or tasteless. Counteract the jaded palate with delicious flavoursome fresh herbs and vegetables.

(v)   Give some thought to what you are hoping to achieve before you offer up a particular dish.

(vi)   Continue to eat out. In chapter 15 we will elaborate upon the type of restaurants to dine in.

Don'ts

(i)   Above all, CookSmart disciples do not simply serve their favourite spag bol *ad nauseam*. Ask a man what his signature dish is and he invariably cites his student special. At a lunch party recently a straw poll of the men revealed that two of them – the husband and a married friend of mine, Greg, owned up to this unsurprising choice. They probably think they can give the celebrated restaurateur Antonio Carluccio a run for his money. Now ask yourself the same question and then reflect how often you dish up the same thing regardless of who is coming for dinner. Quite. You need to be infinitely more cunning. From now on each meal will have to be researched and tailored to match the clientele.

If you are not naturally organised don't worry; you will be making lots of things ahead of time. Best to keep the slog between ourselves.

(ii)   Do not plum bottle. This is going to become something of a mantra. What is a plum bottler? It's like the old adage about the elephant. You will recognise one when you see it. There is a fine line between being the perfect, considerate hostess and being mumsy – warning signs are making marmalade, bottling fruit, even baking cakes. At all stages it is *imperative* to present a youthful, attractive image. A plum bottler is by definition MIDDLE AGED, plump, has greying hair fixed up with a real tortoiseshell hair slide and wears surgical shoes. If the MOD suspects you of PB, next thing he will imagine you in a pair of grey drawers and a pinny. You are toast.

What this means is that even if you can make transparent strudel pastry, you can tell his mum but not let on to the boyfriend. She will be impressed at your homely skills; he will run a mile. It is imperative that you keep your culinary light hidden under a bushel until your mission is complete.

During the courtship phase a man must believe you are far too sophisticated to want to be chained to the stove.

(iii)   One of the key tenets of CookSmart is that, as a 'hip chick' you will never attempt to replicate a dish that can't improve upon a good shop-bought version. Heinz baked beans or tomato soup on Bonfire Night are prime examples. Unless you have a superlative recipe (which I happen to have – see Honeycomb Ice Cream in Chapter 2) forget ice cream making too.

Is this a return to the 1950's?
NO!

Is this self-help manual advocating a return to the stereotypical 1950's domestic slave? Certainly not. The CookSmart discipline is a cerebral one representing the very antithesis of over-boiled and elaborate meals produced by a doormat. And where have we said that we want you to abandon your career? We just want to see you in a long white dress. The only things we want to resuscitate from the '50's era are the fabulously glamorous clothes.

As an aside, offering to roll up your sleeves demonstrates you are well brought up; it is good mannered to reciprocate a man's generosity and dinner dates. Your conduct says you are unafraid of entertaining, someone of substance, not merely 'eye candy'!

There, conscience eased?

We should perhaps say a few words about the 50's since we fear that one or two of your so-called chums (jealous, I bet) will sneeringly remark that cooking in order to get hitched is decidedly old hat or anti-feminist. All you need to say is three important letters please – PMC. Pre-marital cuisine. Like pre-marital sex, PMC undoubtedly happened in a hole-in-the-wall, furtive fashion, in the immediate post-war period. And at the height of the burn-your-bra period. But openly cooking for pleasure by women of all classes in this country is a phenomenon which came out of the closet relatively recently.

Generalising wildly, women in the post war period lived at home with mum and dad before marrying young. Then, before you could say *bouillabaisse*, the gals handed in their notices at work and devoted all day to perfecting a white fish sauce for the Husband. These were housewives in name and in every fibre of their being.

For a case in point, take my mother in law, Hermione. She told me that she did not learn to feed a man at home because her mum had a cook and the first meal she made was on the day she returned from honeymoon. She rang her mother for advice and was instructed to buy two sole, dot them with butter and grill the fish. Hermione then signed up for a Cordon Bleu course, acquired a Constance Fry bible and off she went.

In contrast, modern women marry or partner off much later and stand on their own two feet before they snare a man. Consequently, they have both the means (own flat, kitchen, cooking utensils and knowledge) and opportunity (not living with prying parents) to cook for a suitor. So consider yourself to be not a revisionist, but a leader. We're not advocating a return to domestic drudgery but a little TARGETED cooking to get us what we want.

Who cares about healthy eating before you tie the knot?

"A gourmet who thinks of calories is like a tart who looks at her watch"
James Beard (1903-1985) American restaurateur and food writer.

Back to the business of food. As a CookSmart devotee, flavour is paramount. It is going to be necessary for you to suppress qualms about unhealthy eating (except when entertaining his mum and dad). There will be buckets of double cream, kilos of butter and kegs of salt before you are through.

Get a grip please

Approach food preparation as you would your career. But this is more than your meal ticket for life we are talking about. It is about realising your potential. Mental attitude is key. We want to see you focussed, clear headed, calm. Think of the Dish not first and foremost as friend or lover, but as a prospective client whom you must impress to secure their account.

By analogy, approaching the campaign in a businesslike manner means adopting a 'clean desk policy' on the domestic front. Everyone knows kitchens and bathrooms sell houses. Your loo must be fit for the Queen, towels freshly laundered, not damp from over use. Buy a soap dish and tidy away toiletries. Acne and zit creams must be out of sight. Ditto kids toys/garishly coloured plastic ducks/boats/buckets/Lego pieces. He may know you have kids (he should if you are thinking of him as a prospective husband) but you don't want the chaos of it in his face, when you are trying to relax, lull and soothe him.

In the kitchen, keep serving areas pristine and clutter-free. Hide multipacks of crisps, cheap "value brands", chocolate bars and instant coffee from prying eyes. Lesser mortals than you pig out on unhealthy snacks and instant coffee (conceal the fact that, like me, you guzzle Nescafe Blend 37 and stuff cheese and onion crisps all day). Instead, display an espresso machine or a pretty Italian Bialetti coffee percolator and boxes of sophisticated nibbles. You want him to think of you perched on a stool sipping from a dainty espresso cup, not gulping from a mug with a picture of Bugs Bunny stuffing yourself with Doritos.

Sarah tells me that her father buys loo rolls from ultra-discount outlets like Costco and Macro where you have to buy 800 at a time, or some such massive number. He then piles up the loo rolls on the bathroom window sill so they *almost* obliterate the daylight. If you have to buy cheap or downmarket stuff then hide it out of sight! Very unattractive to guests.

Conceal slog

Confine messy, noisy or convoluted preparative steps to when you are on your own. Men will never understand why a recipe for Thai chicken curry involves sieving redcurrant jelly. Keeping complex preparation work secret adds to your mystique too, making it look like you can create polished dishes without skipping a beat. That's precisely why so many dishes we recommend can be cooked or prepared largely ahead of time (part of the CookSmart ethos).

Do your homework

Learn as much information as you can about The Dish's likes and dislikes. Dear Reader, dig deep. Does he like his *côte de boeuf à point* or bloody? The devil is *in* the detail. Any run-of-the-mill trollop can produce his favourite dish, a grilled beefsteak. But who will know which cut of meat, how to correctly cook it and which wine compliments it perfectly? Is he a rump, sirloin or fillet man? After you have winkled out of him what his favourite dish is, do a dry run on trusted friends before offering it up. But, don't under any circumstances make this beloved fancy until he has sampled a selection of your carefully prepared meals. Cooking his favourite thing on a first date is just too keen/desperate.

One girlfriend of mine who married fairly recently, Caitlin, said that she knew that making her husband gutsy meals played an important part in their courtship because his mother was a competent chef and he eats with gusto. His parents are German and she describes the family cuisine as Westphalian. Lots of stews. She did not seek to emulate this heavy kind of regional fare maybe because she was concerned that she would fall short of his mother's efforts. However, it gave her the idea to put an accent on strong flavours and taste. Interestingly, she suspected that her husband's longstanding ex-girlfriend did not really cook much. So her interest in food gave her a definite edge. Believe me, she can cook!

So, what have you got to offer?

Do you need a spacious, well-equipped handmade Mark Wilkinson kitchen? If you've got one, lucky you. Having a luxurious home is an advantage in the dating stakes. But, the bottom line is no. This epicurean journey is not about producing restaurant-quality food in a state of the art environment. It is about consistently producing the right product, that is, the three T's —Tasty, Timely dishes Tailored to the guest. With good organisation, fine fare is capable of being produced in a kitchen the size of a broom closet.

Now, do you live at home or have a pet? If so, you need to upgrade your circumstance. Living in the same block of flats as your parents is a bad idea since it is difficult to be marriage material if your parents are still running your life. You will need your own place, so go out and rent one.

As for pets, my husband recalls a disastrous evening in New York with a prospective date. He said that the girl's living arrangements put him off. First, her parents lived next door signalling she was still tied to the apron strings. Second, she had a cat which had had its claws taken out so that it would not scratch the furniture. Thirdly, on her fridge was a magnet with the caption, 'the more I know about men, the more I like my cat'.

Stephen interpreted all this as saying that his date found having a relationship with a pet easier to deal with than a man. He decided to leave her to her pussy. (He's not above a Mrs Slocombe-style innuendo.)

Should you splurge on equipment?

We recommend a modest investment in the following essentials.

(1)   Utensils – Top of the list a *bain marie*. I know it sounds complicated, old fashioned and a bit "Victorian Kitchen" but this is just a fancy name for a versatile, heatproof bowl which sits over a saucepan of gently bubbling water. It comes in handy for melting chocolate, making sauces and egg custards and incomparable scrambled eggs (which men love). You don't actually have to buy anything new here, just use a Pyrex or ovenproof bowl over a saucepan (err, you have got a saucepan haven't you? Otherwise this is going to be harder than we thought).

(2)   Equipment – For goodness sake chuck out the ancient kettle you have hawked around since college days. If it's cream with pictures of brown/orange flowers on, then this is especially urgent. Replace it with something cutting edge. I bet yours has never been polished and is clogged up with limescale. It is the one piece of equipment the Dish will use without asking your permission.

(3)   Tableware – throw away tatty table mats with embedded pizza stains. Perhaps you could find some with pictures of cities you want to visit. The image will

be subliminally imprinted on the Dish's mind whenever he looks at them. I know this because my mother in law, Hermione, gave us some mats with pictures of Caribbean islands on them. Now, I long for a rum punch every evening at about 7.30 (well, actually at about 11am. Two noisy tots are enough to drive you to hard liquor).

(4)   Miscellaneous – get a decent pair of scales. The latter is for measuring your weight, not ingredients. This is no time to go up a dress size. Besides, as you get used to the CookSmart technique you will find that you will come to rely less on weights and measures and more on your instincts. Really.

'Desert island discs' store cupboard essentials

Because cooking can be spontaneous it pays to have standby basics in the cupboard. My 'Desert Island Discs' castaway essentials are

- coffee
- garlic
- makeup

Coffee

"When we drink coffee, ideas march in like the army"
Honoré de Balzac (1799-1850)
French novelist and playwright.

For me there is nothing quite so invigorating as a turbo-charged cup of coffee. I can now admit to being an addict. My doctor formed the fantastically unreasonable notion that having in excess of 8 cups a day was not particularly good for me. The meanie rationed me to one cup (well none) and put me on pills for a while. Thank Nescafe Blend 37 for the fact that this learned book was largely completed before I saw the GP. By the way I am down to four a day. Any less and my brain seizes up.

Garlic and fresh herbs

Need we remind you that smell is the most evocative of the senses. Make it work for you. A clever trick is to incorporate herbs/ garlic in as many dishes as possible. Then the MOD will associate delectable aromas with you. Is it an accident I wonder that women were the ones who used to be responsible for tending the herb garden? I think they recognised the importance of controlling foodstuffs with potent, magical properties. Mood influencers.

Why not pick a 'signature' herb? Remember the saying 'Rosemary for remembrance'? Well, *rosmarinus officinalis* is my favourite. Watch what happens when you slip this into the burgers for the lads in Chapter 11.

This green herb, which was introduced to the country by the Romans, has needle-like leaves, is strongly aromatic and suits a broad variety of savoury dishes. Easy to grow provided you have a sunny spot, you can have it permanently on hand. I have a large bush outside my kitchen window where it is accessible.

Turning to garlic, I have never been sure about whether *allium sativum* is a herb or a vegetable since it is a member of the onion family. Who cares? Throw in as much garlic as you like petal. Since ancient times cooks have used this pungent stuff to embolden cuisine. Even Pharaohs had garlic-infused meals for the afterlife. It is guaranteed to lend a certain *je ne sais quoi* to what you make. Buy industrial quantities. It is so indispensable that we are going to rate dishes which contain this potent ingredient on a scale from 1 to 5. The 'vampire rating' will denote the garlic content to shoot for.

I should mention that some dullards – in my opinion uninformed people – believe that garlic breath throws a dampener on romance. It owes its robust aroma to its sulphurous properties. These folks are probably the same ones who don't like to go abroad because they distrust foreign food. One person I know springs to mind automatically. Jenny is happier pottering about in a Pacamac in a rain-swept English coastal resort like Mevagissey (a very pretty place mind you, where you can buy the ultimate Cornish pasty) than taking the risk of getting the runs from eating pasta vongole in Verona. She thinks she has a delicate constitution. We are cut from different cloth. Do not be put off please. Provided the two of you are both eating the same thing the MOD will not notice garlic unduly – if he does I'll let you in on a secret – I read that chewing on a sprig of parsley is supposed to help. I have not tried this. Frankly, love, I'd stick to scrubbing your teeth and eating peppermints.

PS – if he really does not like garlic you are well and truly stuffed. We suggest you throw away this book immediately. You will be on your own kid!

Other herbs
We would have suggested that you tie up home made *bouquet garnis* – bundles of fresh herbs (parsley, thyme and bay leaves are the traditional triumvirate) but this is a tad Plum Bottley. The advantage of herbs such as rosemary, basil and garlic is that only two hand actions are required – chopping and throwing into the pan.

Make up
Like unflavoured food there are few women lucky enough to look great 'au naturel'. Always keep a bag with mascara, powder and lipgloss in the food cupboard so that you can refresh your face when the Dish is relaxing on the sofa in the sitting room awaiting your next masterpiece.

PS why haven't we mentioned alcohol?
Believe me, we have plenty to say about your boozing habits in Chapter 2. For now all we would mention is by all means have a bottle of French white on ice, but champagne either looks a tad desperate or worse (if you are thinking of a long-term catch). It makes you look like a heavy-drinking party girl. This is out of keeping with the slightly aloof got-it-together image you need to cultivate *à la* Greta Garbo.

White lies

Look, I am a firm believer in the truth. You may remember that I once worked as a lawyer. I could probably still recite *verbatim* the oath you give before offering evidence in court. But, you would never tell a girlfriend shortly before her wedding that she is fat, you can't stand her fiancé and that she is making a big mistake. So, some untruths are palatable. And I am going to suggest one little fib.

We have established that Plum Bottling activities are verboten. But what could be the harm of inventing an innocuous 'Bunbury' of our own? This was Algernon Moncrieff's fictional friend in Oscar Wilde's *The Importance of Being Earnest*. He constantly used the excuse of having to go and visit his sick friend, where he was really off to have a good time.

This culinary battle would be easier to fight using top of the range weapons. Would it really matter if you conjured up (a more user-friendly term than fabricated) an aunt or close friend of the family – we could call her Aunt Jessica. We could attribute to her all those delectable essentials we can't have him knowing that you made. Otherwise he might decide you are a bit 1950's housewife, mumsy and doormatty. So, tell him Aunt Jessica made those mince pies, onion marmalade, pickled apricots and anything else that is credibly transportable from her thatched cottage to your flat. Are we *ad idem* (in agreement) then? Good.

Etiquette

If you wish to be treated as a lady, behave in a refined manner. Ditch unappetising habits such as scraping saucepans and licking the spoon or eating cold sausages with fingers. At least, when the Dish is around.

Don't be a mug

Unless you are rich or very beautiful – or both - I think men *are* seduced by shallow superficial glitz which can be achieved by little things *cuisiniere* such as your choice of wine (See Chapter 2) or cups with saucers versus mugs. We certainly are. The latter are the equivalent of stockings versus tights or first class tickets versus economy. Small details are make or break. Pour milk into a jug before putting it on the table, sugar in a bowl with a small spoon. This may seem, as we've said before, old-fashioned, but well brought-up men like to see things looking nice and not like a transport caff.

The jury is out on whether ketchup bottles should be seen on the dinner table. It is axiomatic that this would not happen at a formal dinner party.

But for breakfast why not? It shows that you can relax but please do not decant the ketchup or brown sauce into a bowl. That is just plain naff.

Tuck in today, restrain yourself from pigging out tomorrow

Always serve yourself an adequate portion, including carbohydrates. It is better to leave food uneaten than sit nibbling a leaf while the MOD is tucking into a substantial meal. You must show that you have a healthy appetite and are unconcerned about your weight. Being calorie-obsessed will be a red flag!

By analogy, dieting will be seriously boring. It also suggests it is only a matter of time before you balloon. If your perfect figure seems to be all natural, requiring no hard work to keep in shape, he will believe you will remain this way.

What's more, even if he has a tum like a pregnant hedgehog, the last thing he wants is to be press-ganged into joining your diet. So, do not let on either that you know exactly how many calories are in a doughnut. In case there is any misunderstanding, this is not about having to be a size zero but rather about not being suspected of having zero confidence in your current form.

And finally – the SCORE?

Let me spell it out. We believe in 'results' dishes. So should you. You will see that at the end of each meal/chapter we will have a review of what you have achieved under the heading 'SCORE'. There will be three categories with marks to be awarded out of ten. They are:

i.   Commitment – this is how much you have increased his thinking of you as marriage (or long term partner) material.

ii.   Romance – ahem – he'll demonstrate how much more desirable/sexy he finds you!

iii.   Fun – did you have a laugh or was it a struggle?

I don't think we have left anything important out, have we? We are going to give you our score. Let us know how you get on at our website: www.thedishbook.co.uk.

Right, now you have the basic facts under your belt, shall we proceed to the first and perhaps the most significant meal you will ever make?

chapter 1

Establishing base camp
The ultimate first meal

'A *noble dish*'
William Makepeace Thackeray (1811-1863)
English novelist

Inspiration

Think Lauren Bacall in *Key Largo*. She got Bogart. Serenely sophisticated. Let's see if you can have a go at this shall we?

It would be natural to suffer 'first night nerves' when you are getting ready to treat the Dish to a home-cooked meal for the first time. A million thoughts will naturally cross your mind; what you should make being top of the list.

You will fall flat on your face if you do any of the following:

• Make romantic food. This means no oysters. Definitely no heart-shaped pizza. I have to live with the

1

shame of making this for a beau, Ben, when I was 24. I wondered if the cad let on about this to one of his friends since I always felt I was a laughing stock amongst his close pals.

- Prepare a dish which your mum would advise you to make. Like over-poached salmon with lemon sauce. Yes, the twerp that I was when I did not know any better served this one up to Ben too. He went on to marry a tall, beautiful and confident-looking blonde, Vicky, who probably knew what the aspiring wife of a city lawyer should order when dining at the super deluxe hotel *Das Grand Hotel Zermatterhof* in Switzerland. Sea bass and fruit plate. At that point, I suspect I would have bombed by choosing heavy peasant fare like Wiener schnitzel and rosti followed by chocolate pudding. I *still* would, come to think of it.

- Cook student fare: Chilli con carne, Spag Bol etc. This will remind the MOD of his first love. He needs to look forward, not back.

- Serve strongly-flavoured ethnic food if you want romance – unless of course you are both used to it. What goes in one end must come out the other, not to put too fine a point on it!

But do you prepare the sort of meal he would have at a favourite haunt like *The Ivy* or, at one of the funkier, more modern places you prefer? Like *Zuma* or *Nobu* in London. All these eateries could be booked up for months in advance. Only 'A' listers might conceivably get in at the last minute, so you won't.

As it happens a great friend of mine shared a name with a famous politician. (My friend would probably say he was well known in his own right). *Whatever.* We ate out a lot a few years back and whenever I rang *The Ivy* for a table for the two of us we were always accommodated. They were charming when we turned up but the phalanx of photographers disappointingly took no interest at all. I secretly long to appear on the front page under the caption *'society beauty dines with mystery guest at one of London's hot spots'*.

Restaurants must be used to disappointments. The husband also once booked a table for a large party at *Quaglino's* and mentioned that his clients were expecting the Russian Ambassador to join them for lunch. I was seated next to the guest of honour and tried to engage his interest on the subject of anti-dumping legislation but surprisingly he did not really seem interested in what I had to say. It was not just because this was stultifying tedious. Echoing Gogol's famous play *'The Government Inspector'* in which an entire town kow-tows to a nobody they mistake for an important official, it transpired that the man tucking into his oysters was about twelve rungs below ambassadorial level, possibly just above cleaning staff.

Back to your predicament. Will the Dish think you are a prat if you can only boil an egg? Well, frankly, yes. We would be lying if we said this would impress the fellow. So, will we let you chicken out with some wet excuse that you are working late and allow you to make a reservation instead? NO, NO, NO. It is far too late to turn back now. You have paid for this book so you may as well see if this formula works. In any event, going back to what I said before about the rich and famous, unless you have a megastar relative it is way too late to get in anywhere half decent.

Our advice to you is to grit your teeth and get stuck in. You said you enjoyed a challenge when you went for the last job interview. And this is what they mean. Sharpen those knives. This meal represents the crossing of the Rubicon. Execute it well and Rome ought to be within your sights. Fail, and it will be you who is renewing her cable TV subscription. But, Sarah and I are going to hold your little hand as we waltz through this virgin territory together.

Now for the meat. What is the right meal for the occasion?

Your Opening Gambit for the hungry Man of Your Dreams

Rare Chateaubriand* with jacket potato, sour cream, fresh chives and roasted tomato served with freshly prepared mustard in a proper mustard pot	**Vampire rating 3** *This should be cooked rare unless he insists on it being well done. Only use vine ripened tomatoes.
Peche melba	Fresh peaches are essential.
Freshly brewed coffee	Remember mugs are history/strictly for you on your own, builders, the cleaning lady and The Lads – see Chapter 11.
Wine	Volnay or any other good red Burgundy.
Ambiance	Opera –Verdi's La Traviata. Leave a copy of the Royal Opera House programme on the coffee table and rumple it to look as if you have read it. You could also put your name down on the waiting list for Glyndebourne. Then you will receive regular free newsletters and programmes but you will not need to commit to a membership fee for about 25 years by which time we hope you will have found someone to fork out for it.
Dress code	Not office attire, no jeans unless you are over 5'11". Think tarty but don't overdo the make up. Perfume – no 'elevator gagging' scent - *only* Chanel No5. Think of those Nicole Kidman adverts.
Conversation	No romantic or sentimental gushy drivel.

4

Look, duckie, we are even going to spell out what wine you need to serve. Trust me, this king of Pinot Noirs will demonstrate you know something about wine. It is delicious by the way.

Why opera? Operatic music projects a classical image of a woman who understands and appreciates elegance. Make sure that you buy a full opera not a high street compilation! It will need to be a light opera as this is background music so it is best to stick to anything in Italian.

How do I make this supper perfectly? Stop panicking. We will talk you through this one.

The main course

Relax! Have we mentioned yet that you will need to ration your drink tonight when He arrives? We *cannot* have you getting sloshed before you serve the meal. One quick sharpener only. What could appeal more to the masculine palate and be more mouth-watering than perfect beef fillet accompanied by vegetables that a man actually wants to eat? This is gutsy, simple fare.

The first meal is pivotal to success. It needs to establish that you can provide a man with what he likes. No more, no less. The extra level of detail you go to is vital and will not go unnoticed.

- No attempt to ram three kinds of superfluous greenery down the poor man's throat.

- Proper mustard in a mustard pot. It does not matter if He prefers French. You are showing that you are classy enough to serve the real thing.

- Meat uncomplicated by any sauce. Prince Philip apparently once said '*I never see any home cooking. All I get is fancy stuff*'. He would love this dinner.

Buy the best cut of meat that you can find and make sure that it is aged. It is a simple fact that good cuts of meat are tenderised by the ageing process. But, do not worry: it is not that long a period. Many supermarkets now have aged beef as part of their range.

If you do not enjoy beef (I do not, so you would be in good company) choose a slice of fresh tuna for yourself. This can be roasted simultaneously, but in a separate dish. Dependent upon thickness, the tuna steak should take no more than 10 mins to roast. You must explain that you do not like beef to reassure him that it is ok for him to eat red meat with you.

The reason we have plumped for *Côte de boeuf* over ordinary steak is that the former is a more reliable dish to get right. Indeed, steak looks and smells better if it is charred on a barbie. Even if you slightly overcook a fillet you can slice off the outside and the middle should be fine.

Most people would associate steak- type meals with chips. But, the last thing you want to do is to be standing over a deep-fat fryer cooking his blessed fries. You will smell like a chip shop and will lose any chance for romance later in the evening. Plus your face sweats up when standing over all that greasy steam – not a good first-date look.

hot drinks

Round the meal off with real, not decaffeinated, coffee - for him. Weak coffee will undermine the favourable impression you have built up so far. Practice making a good strong brew and serve it with amaretto biscuits. Any type of Italian biscotti in fact will make you look more sophisticated than if you offer him a packet of digestives.

However much you love coffee, for appearance's sake, please do not have some. It would look more ladylike, more *Bacallesque*, at this time of night if you drank a cup of herbal tea or hot water with a slice of lemon.

Now is not the time – but on another more perfect evening, as you will see, we are going to surprise your bloke by making a pot of mint tea. This is incredibly easy – just infuse (aka leave to soak) some mint leaves in a tea pot with hot water for a few minutes having dunked an ordinary teabag in it for a *few seconds*. According to one of my neighbours, Naomi, this is the secret to a perfect brew. She ought to know since her mother has a flat in Jerusalem where I imagine they knock this back by the quart in summertime. If he has a sweet tooth, stir in a couple of teaspoons of sugar.

PS. Finally, remember this is a performance to show your competence at managing an event. Clear up soiled dishes etc as you go along and pack them immediately into a dishwasher, if you have one, or into the sink where they must be washed up when the meal is over. If this is a mid-week dinner, thank him but politely decline his offer to help dry up since he has been working all day.

Manage ok did you? Course you did.

SCORE

It is time to add it up.

1. Commitment	5	There is no question this will have got him thinking in the right direction.
2. Romance	7	If he does not oblige tonight by at least showing his ardour ask yourself if you are backing the right horse.
3. Fun	2	This was a nervy evening for you. Don't worry, it will get easier.

chapter 2

Consolidating your position
Five perfect follow-up suppers *à deux*

"There is no love sincerer than the love of food"
Man and Superman (1903)
George Bernard Shaw (1856-1950) Irish playwright

Inspiration
Grace Kelly in *Rear Window*. Poised, elegant and unfazed by taking on a minor royal family and small principality.

Hang on a minute. What happens if the Dish finds out about this tome? He won't. Men are not like us. They are uncomplicated machines born largely without a curiosity gene. You won't find one poking around drawers hoping to find something interesting about you. But, you might as well not draw attention to this book, so stick it in with your knickers.

I bet you breathed a huge sigh of relief when the thank you text arrived three days after your 'base camp' success. Fifteen love.

He might be thrilled to bits but we are not. Naturally, we congratulate you on reaching this stage, but complacency is premature. You should remember that a past achievement is just that – past. A cook is only as good as her last meal. The task now is to entrench your position by maintaining the MOD's expectations so that he realises that you are no culinary one night stand.

We have devised a series of competent suppers for him to get his teeth into when it is just the two of you. They will include an eclectic variety of foodstuffs, a deliberate ploy to make him perceive you as being cosmopolitan and interesting. The main courses in particular will be packed with robust flavours, so this is going to be a baptism of fire with the CookSmart approach.

What's more, homemade food is going to be a breath of fresh air after all that fussy overpriced slop he has had too much of in restaurants with other girlfriends he's been dating. Hopefully your cooking talents will distinguish you from the pack. Remember you need the others to look grabbing and ungrateful. What's more, your sense of thrift will be particularly appealing these days with the FTSE yo-yoing – along with his promotion prospects.

But don't go overboard on the food front. It would be overkill if you were to serve superior nosh every day. Ration these substantial delights to say, one a week. The idea is to *gradually* introduce your man to the concept of being indulged. In time, if he gets pleasure from your efforts he will begin to look forward to your next creation.

On other days:

• Make him wonderful light meals (see Chapter 9)

• Make yourself scarce – work late/go out with friends/take up tennis/badminton/Mandarin and, here's the fun part - make sure that there is nothing tasty in the fridge. If he stays over the odd night, or has even moved in (you work fast girl, we like your style) he must be left to fend for himself. Better still, make sure there is a loaf of stale bread and two tins of cheap supermarket salmon. No mayonnaise. See if he can make a meal out of that.

• Do not be afraid to buy in quality take-aways – Indian, Chinese, fish and chips. Not chain pizza.

• Eat out as usual.

One moment please... Do you mind if I bring up a few little things before you roll up your sleeves again?

Dearest Reader, before we set you free to embark upon this next phase, we would suggest you first take on board some sound advice which will assist you in responding to *all* the tasks that lie ahead of you in this and the succeeding chapters.

1. Practicalities

Because cooking may take place *chez lui* it would be prudent to familiarise yourself with the MOD's kitchen. This is a fantastic excuse to nose around, which you are probably dying to do, aren't you? I remember in the honeymoon period of getting to know my husband I chanced upon a missive from a former girlfriend, Tabitha, in the pan cupboard! Do you think I opened it – illiterate romantic twaddle. She gained the nick name, 'Teapot'. Try and maintain focus. You should be checking that he has such basic ingredients as pepper, fresh garlic and a chopping board. Any extraneous finds are a bonus.

Does he own oven gloves and an apron? Unlikely perhaps in a bachelor pad. However, you cannot buy any kitchen equipment for a man. He will feel threatened. Make do with what there is.

Under no circumstances should you take your own stuff to his home. Some women adopt a continuous 'drop by' policy for their kit. It probably starts with lingerie. Fairly soon they will be trying to take root with all manner of clothes, deodorant and an Imelda Marcos collection of shoes. Men can see this ruse a mile off and don't like it. We will not need this. You are going to get in through the front door.

2. Venue and accoutrements

First things first, decide where to eat. It really does not matter if you dine in the kitchen, dining room or sitting room cum dining area. The key is to sit at a table, not on your lap in front of *Coronation Street*. This will make it clear to the Dish that you are civilised and not a slob. Well, all right, make an exception if you want to watch a key episode of *24* or anything with Rupert Penry-Jones, formerly of 'Spooks' fame. I am not sure I am ever going to get over him being killed. For sure that programme's dead in our household.

Sarah has a very nice a single girlfriend who seems to virtually live in her bedroom, although she has a perfectly good living/dining room. She suspects Amanda eats in the bedroom, watches TV there, makes all her phone calls there. This is fine if you are on your own (nice idea and quiet relaxing I should think) but, inviting a *man* to dine in your boudoir could give the wrong message, even if it is on the sofa, and might make you look like a hermit/weirdo, not she hastens to add, that Amanda does this. USE the dining table!

Now, what if he wants to watch something on telly at supper time? Go out. Otherwise this could set a dangerous precedent. Men can be childlike. I have unwisely started to let my small daughter, eat supper on a tray in front of The *Numberjacks*. Consequently, I have to bribe her back to the table when her father is in the house. He has threatened to put us both on the 'naughty step' if he catches us.
Sarah says ditto – her husband doesn't want kiddies' crumbs/sauce

splatters on the sofa and doesn't understand it sometimes makes for a quiet life if you let them eat in front of the TV.

Make sure you have correctly positioned the cutlery at each setting. The *hors d'oeuvre* implements are of course on the outside. Dessert spoons and forks go at a horizontal above the plate, napkins on the left. *Just checking* to see if you were paying attention. The napkin goes on the right. Only PB's would use carefully pressed linen napkins every day. Good quality white or cream paper napkins are best since these colours are not gauche. It would be trashy to substitute napkins with sheets of kitchen towel. Even worse, a bog roll shoved on the table!

Having candles would also be a grave mistake, girls. They are overtly romantic and will pressurise the MOD – they practically shout, '*I feel romantic, do you?*' It is for him to dictate the pace on seduction. Your job is to make him appreciate you. Limit candles to a formal dinner party setting and rely instead on the subtlety of mood lighting to create a more intimate, but less in-your-face romantic ambiance. If the overhead lights are too harsh – fluorescent strips lend a particularly unforgiving pallor and can make a room feel like a holding cell at the police station – pick up a couple of table lamps, again in non-offensive, neutral colours.

3. The demon drink

As this is business, you will need to keep a clear head during the execution of meals. Never forget that you want the MOD to see you as someone who enjoys herself, but not as a lush.

Do's and don'ts with booze

> '*Compromises are for relationships, not for wine*'
> Pliny the Elder (AD23-AD79) Roman author and
> naturalist philosopher.

Even if you can hold your drink and were the only one in your party the police let go outside *Boujis* (the beautiful people's London nightclub) last summer, ration yourself to a couple of glasses. Getting tanked up repels some nice men who might prefer more ladylike behaviour in a wife. I suspect two women I have met squandered their chances in part because they should have exercised greater restraint at all times. One was stunning. Had she imbibed less and cooked more I can't help but think she would have landed a jet-setting mover and shaker who could have kept her in Zac Posen frocks for life. I have an image of the second woman, glassy eyed, at a 'posh do', umpteenth champagne glass in one hand, fag in the other, with her soon to be ex-boyfriend looking on in obvious distaste.

How you come across also depends on what kind of a drunk you are – if you're a happy drunk, its fine to get a bit merry once in a while. If you're an aggressive, depressive, overbearing, hectoring bore, then you know what to do. Let him see those sides of you later...

Instead, why not make a white wine spritzer and ensure there are plenty of bottles of mineral water in the fridge? Keep to one brand. Perrier in *glass* bottles looks and tastes good.

This brings us neatly onto the choice of wine. ***Time to come out of the bush.*** It is fashionable for many women to order New World and, in particular, Australian Chardonnays, and no doubt they are quality wines. *That is beside the point.* This exercise is all about projecting an image so why not make it exclusively French? More sexy Catherine Deneuve and less Dame Edna. Surely you can see how much more sophisticated you are going to look by always choosing *la vraie* France. Think of this range; Burgundy, Bordeaux, Côtes du Rhone, Beaujolais – a chateau here, a chateau there! Each dish we have selected has been married to a delicious and classy French *vin*. Ooo la la!

Whilst the writers love French alcohol, champagne must not be bought. This is nectar of the Gods but it has celebratory connotations. Like jewellery, we feel it is something a man should pay for.

What is the best drink to start off an evening? Whilst you might be tempted to offer the Dish a cocktail the problem is that you would be expected to join him in what is likely to be rocket fuel. A vodka martini, shaken but not stirred, is liable to leave you flattened on an empty stomach and hence incapable of carrying out your mission. There is also a danger of a James Bond cliché.

You don't want to be seen slurping a pina colada either - complete with mini parasol and cherry!

Be smart. Probe discreetly to discover what the MOD's favourite beer is and stock up the fridge.

To win a few more brownie points, go to the trouble of making a few tasty tit bits. This will keep him going until supper time. To make an easy *canapé*, take a slice of salami and top it with a piece of Emmenthal on toasted, buttered rye bread, cut into four to make bite sized morsels. Alternatively, try soft goat's cheese with a thin sliver of tomato on rough Scottish oat cakes. Thick chunks of tomato have an unpleasant habit of sliding off onto a man's shirt or his best Kenzo tie. Tip : designer neckwear is bound to have been a present from an ex and he will be livid.

Only make snacks with tapenade if you know the MOD likes black olives. The tastiest olive paste is homemade, but this is too PB for present purposes.

4. Marlboro man

What if the Dish is a two pack a day man? No easy response to this even if you like the occasional puff too. Assess the objective. It must be to let the Dish know that you will not stand in his way when there is something he enjoys but you have concerns for his health. In reality you could not care less if he smokes himself to death unless he can deliver. What you are doing is seeking to navigate a fine line between caring and allowing him a free rein.

Nevertheless, the MOD should be asked to refrain from smoking at mealtimes and in your house. Unfortunately, if he will not accede to this reasonable request you should seriously ask yourself if this person deserves you.

Assuming the MOD is considerate you can win points by showing your attention for detail. After dinner, calmly produce a cigarette box containing his favourite brand along with a decent lighter and a proper ashtray. Preferably something which has not been whipped from a local restaurant or a fancy London eaterie such as Quaglino's where the tables used to have those attractive Q shaped ashtrays. I suppose though, that since the smoking ban, ashtrays are a thing of the past. I must seriously get out more and investigate this point – for research you understand.

Your grandparents probably have a 1950's ashtray you could trouser. Only please do not let on it is a family heirloom. Sentiment will not work on the MOD. But, if you really don't want your home stinking, don't be browbeaten and get him to go out into the garden/balcony. I would not bank on this romance, incidentally.

5. Timing

When the hunter returns from the modern jungle he needs food. Serve supper without too great a delay even if you have taken the edge off his hunger with the canapés.

6. Boring points about menu content

We will be as short as we can. Read this and you will understand why so many men are prescribed statin tablets in later life to keep their cholesterol levels under control.

Greenery

Men don't like it and they are not interested in getting their 'five a day.' It is important though to serve something with the meat, for the sake of form. The only greens they will be interested in are at the golf club. Needless to say, there should be no frozen peas or other boring school dinner type veg. I have one friend, Timothy, who does not do what he calls *'squishy'* food – most cooked vegetables and fruit in fact. I wonder if he would have scurvy if he never drank red wine?

Salad

Ditto above. Forget it unless you are a supermodel in which case he will be happy to watch you eating a solitary sprig of rocket all day. Salad is a woman's thing. It's low-cal and light so men aren't interested.

Cooked vegetables

Cooked vegetables must be prepared *al dente* and have proper flavour.

Do any of these ideas grab you?

Roasted beetroot?	Unless you have a good cleaning lady, never cut or peel beetroot on a wooden work surface because the juice is a devil to clean. Ditto red cabbage. Sorry to bring this up but beets turn your wee red. After serving this to one guest, the poor man was convinced he had a terminal illness and was referred to a specialist for an ultrasound of his intestine! Sarah was scared witless when this happened to her too.
Broad beans?	This is excellent bonding fodder. If he is the kind of man who likes to do things with his hands, shell fresh beans/peas together. Caitlin (Greg's wife) says that preparing food brought her and her boyfriend (now husband) closer. Worth trying once. This tack will not work with everyone. Be careful; any attempt by my husband and me to share kitchen space has led to threats of divorce within five minutes.

	Don't misunderstand please. Stevie baby wants to strut his stuff in the kitchen but just *not at the same time* as me. Interestingly, although he obviously appreciates her cooking skills, Sarah's husband Peter only wants to be called to table *once* everything is ready. To be fair, he will clear away or load the dishwasher but he does NOT want to cook! Boil the broad beans, then eat warm or cold with a decent splash of white wine vinegar and extra virgin oil.
Corn on the cob?	Only make this if there is dental floss in the house. The kernels have a horrid habit of getting stuck between the teeth.
Cauliflower?	Don't bother unless smothered in a garlicky cheese sauce with a **Vampire rating 3**
Braised gem lettuce	Now, has it ever occurred to you to gently cook little lettuces in a smidgen of butter and black pepper?

Soups

A short word about these is all that is warranted. Only PBs make soup. Buy it in.

There is, in any event, a time and place for soup but this is limited. Heinz tomato soup is a must for Bonfire Night or an autumn picnic. Accordingly, unless the MOD has a particular love of *potage* (my husband unfortunately does, and so for some reason do most Russians) I would not dream of serving it. It is a pity to squander the MOD's appetite on something he could buy from the supermarket.

Now, whet his appetite for you with these meals.

Menu 1 Preferably for a balmy summer's evening mid week

Tapas	Choose a selection of dishes from the following:
Ready made	Chorizo sausages ready cooked, Serrano ham with sliced mango, large green olives, cooked prawns – you will need to squeeze over lime/lemon juice and add some chopped coriander.
To be made	Herbed chick peas (ie chick peas doused in oil and vinegar, cumin, garlic and some sort of fresh green herb). **Vampire rating 1**; green beans poached for no more than 2 mins dressed with oil and flaked dried chillies; chargrilled red peppers with skins removed and marinated in oil and white wine vinegar; cous cous with broad beans and coriander; baby new potato salad. **Vampire rating 2**
Honeycomb Ice Cream	Yummy – we are letting you in on a secret (see recipe later).
Wine	Crozes Hermitage or any other red Rhone, or make a jug of Sangria.
Ambiance	1960's classics; Like the Doors or the Rolling Stones.
Dress Code	Feminine but not frills or flowers. Avoid Flamenco dresses despite the Spanish theme. They remind one of Barbie dolls. Lots of bangles but only for the wrist. PS in summer for goodness sake paint your toe nails if your feet are going to be on display. What colour? It does not matter. Remember that chipped varnish looks slutty so always have some remover in the bathroom.
Any other points?	Eat *al fresco* if you can with outdoor lanterns to capture that holiday feeling.
Conversation	Be nonchalant about your plans for the summer holidays.

Music

Too much classical music and he will think you are old fashioned and square. '60's rock bands are timeless and a bit more fun.

The food

The tapas theme is going to be a lively choice because there is the element of surprise attached to it.

- Every dish is packed with interesting flavours.
- Each one can be prepared in advance.
- Avoid this menu if he has just returned from a trip to Spain or if his mum is called Paloma.

We suggest you eat this mid-week because I try to avoid buying shellfish on Sundays or Mondays. Please, if anyone out there works/is married to someone in the fishing industry could they enlighten me as to whether it is a myth that fishermen don't work on the day of the Lord so fish can't possibly be fresh at the beginning of the week?

My husband would be crestfallen if I did not mention his cooking once. Let's get it over and done with. Stephen is not a bad cook but he tends to leave the kitchen looking like the Somme. He is normally banned from making anything. I have ungraciously conceded though, that my potato salad is inferior to his. Not surprisingly I had never heard of anyone including spring onion. We made two large bowls of this as part of a buffet for my parents' Golden Wedding lunch party to see which one was most popular. His was. Stephen's view is that men (who were the ones largely eating this) do not usually worry about breathing onion fumes over everyone.

You will see in a short while that there is one man who will be concerned about this.

Happy now, darling?

Honeycomb ice cream

I IMPLORE YOU TO MAKE THIS. And I'm even going to give you the recipe. As for the dessert, the MOD will not have experienced anything as uniquely fabulous as this ice cream. He will be in *Nirvana*.

Introduced to me by a glamorous, incredibly nice (and thankfully, married) cousin, Ingrid – one of the few people in London who hosts sensational dinner parties (nibbles, three courses with everyone dressed up to the nines) I briefly believed that my husband would seriously consider exchanging me for her on the strength of this dessert.

This is one of *only* two occasions on which I have rung someone for a recipe. Apparently I was not the only one. The other was for a sensational radicchio salad which I was served on New Year's Eve by Caitlin, now firmly one of my new best friends. Never pass up the chance to find an eye-opening starter. As an aside, it is amazing how quickly like minded women buddy up. See more on this in Chapter 4.

Now, I promised myself I would not get bogged down in recipes but I am prepared to relent ONCE. Because you have decided to go with us on this odyssey.

Ingredients
1 tablespoon golden syrup, 2 ½ tablespoons caster sugar, ½ teaspoon bicarbonate of soda, 284 ml double cream whipped to soft peaks, small tin condensed milk

This is ridiculously easy to make so it does not fall foul of the Plum Bottling rule. And it has a grown-up flavour unlike vanilla and chocolate. Not having to use a cumbersome ice cream maker is a big plus too. Get this out and your man will be heading for the door. He will think you are practicing for his kids. Scary.

Method
Grease a sheet of baking parchment/paper. Gently heat the sugar

and syrup in a saucepan to boiling point. Boil for 3 mins stirring frequently. Turn off the heat. Add the bicarbonate of soda. The mixture will froth up like a witch's brew. You may wish to use oven gloves in case it spits. Pour immediately onto the greased sheet spreading it thinly and allow to cool and harden. This takes a few minutes. The saucepan will need to be soaked.

Meanwhile incorporate the condensed milk into the whipped cream. Break up the honeycomb into tiny pieces and add to the cream. I know that it is incredibly tempting to try honeycomb when it has set but beware, it can be quite hard on its own. This could break teeth! Let the mixture stand for 10 mins before freezing. I find that this softens the honeycomb a bit. It is therapeutic to hit the honeycomb with a rolling pin. Cover it first so splinters don't go everywhere.

Remove the ice cream from the freezer 20 mins before you need it.

Menu 2 For a Sunday lunch

Now, moving on to your next challenge, you should make what we call 'serious food' to prove that you have depth. A French classic. This will put him in the mood for whisking you off for a weekend to Paris. Have some Eurostar timetables lying about and quiz any French friends about where to stay. A Novotel is unlikely to be conducive to romance.

I adore the *Abbé St Germain* a stone's throw from St Surplice on the Left Bank. Cosier (and vastly cheaper) than the Ritz. I was recommended this boutique hotel by a colleague some years ago. I particularly like the way the white-gloved waiter served G&T on room service with a tray of nibbles. There's a sweet courtyard too where breakfast is served in summer. For other meals, since there is no restaurant, head down Rue Cassette about fifty yards to possibly the world's best bistro.

The unspoken dress code for this city hotel is smart continental –

lots of cream and high heels and groomed hair – and you will be
embarrassed if some people you know who are also in town pitch
up in matching unisex-style high-cut shorts and garish Hawaiian
patterned shirts. I certainly was.

Duck cassoulet with braised lettuce	**Vampire rating 6!** Do not skimp on the ingredients. This must contain cannellini beans, Toulouse sausages (ah- pure garlic heaven), bacon or pancetta as well as duck. Go easy on the tinned toms otherwise your sauce might be too diluted. As in the next menu, it is advisable to use wine (here white) plus a modest quantity of chicken stock to keep the meat from drying out in the oven.
Baked banana with a cardamom and orange sauce (simmer orange juice with a spoonful of sugar, bashed seeds of 12 pods and a slurp of brandy).	Delicious with a spoonful of crème fraiche or vanilla ice cream.
Wine	Cotes du Luberon or other regional red.
Ambiance	Edith Piaf or any other French crooner.
Dress Code	Casual but not sloppy. How about a nice short skirt if your legs are good. No peasant smocks, boob tubes or trackie bottoms
Any other points?	Make sure you have the Sunday Times. Men like to read the sport and boring financial bits.
Conversation	Read the headlines yourself so at least you will know who we are at war with and which party is in power.

Music
This choice is pretty obvious.

I associate duck with the south west of France, in particular with towns like Carcassonne and Montpelier, gastronomic havens where *quack quack* dishes feature on many menus. Perhaps it is no coincidence that you find so many polished brass plaques of liver specialists in the doorways.

Duck casserole is an ideal meal on a cold winter's day when the MOD has returned from prancing about a football pitch freezing his balls off and pretending to be David Beckham. This *pot au feu* has a peasant earthiness to it. While taking a shower, he will savour the pungent wafts of garlicky meat. You will have seen that this has a high vampire rating.

On a practical level, the casserole keeps well and improves in fact, if it is left to sit overnight in the fridge. It can therefore be made a day in advance and slowly reheated in the oven. A CookSmart trick.

Menu 3 For a Friday night

Roast shoulder of lamb with a garlic, butter, porridge oats, honey, mustard and rosemary crust, potatoes dauphinoise, honey parsnips and peas	**Vampire rating 3** Shovel in the garlic! Bring peas to life by serving them with torn mint leaves.
Cherry clafoutis	Use fresh or morello cherries.
Wine	Any claret, preferably St Julien.
Ambiance	A fun jazz compilation; nothing too discordant.

Dress Code	Slinky with heels. How about getting a sophisticated bob? Make sure your eyebrows are defined too. Hairy yaks are less alluring than groomed goddesses.
Any other points?	1. This is the beginning of the weekend so why not kickstart things with a fantastically delicious Caipirinia – (you need aqua diente, cane sugar rum- Oddbins sell it). 2. Remember to use table lamps rather than overhead lighting.
Conversation	Concentrate on stringing a sentence together since Caipirinias are heady stuff.

Music

I know we said you should not buy an opera compilation. Jazz is different – unless he is an anorak he is unlikely to have any knowledge of individual artists so a funky compilation particularly with sax should do. Nothing too depressing, as jazz can be!

This is the meal to make on a Friday night after a long week at the office. What better way to make him relax than to serve a satisfyingly large dinner.

The cunning aspect of this meal is that you will be able to capitalise on the MOD's existing goodwill towards people who make him a roast – MUM.

All men like to gorge themselves on roast meat and have misty-eyed memories of the Sunday lunch *en famille*. They may even still dutifully return to the fold every week. It would not be uncommon if there is a reverential, bordering on religious, association in his mind between the roast *mit all ze trimmings* and family life.

We would like you to recreate this meal with a superior version if you can. For example, Mum's gravy might be Bisto! Trump this with a gutsy mustard rosemary herb crust for lamb or honey lemon sauce for chicken. But, importantly, try to serve this in the week only and be casual about any praise you receive. Hopefully, the MOD will deduce that he will only get the full Monty on the proper day when he has left his bachelor days behind him.

This lamb hits all the right notes with carnivores. It would present as a confident dish made by someone unafraid of bold flavours. It slots into the CookSmart mould perfectly, since you can adapt the ingredients for the herb crust to suit your taste. It is difficult to botch.

Making a thick outer coating helps keep the meat succulent and infuses the cooking juices with extra oomph. Versatile as well, it will not embarrass at lunch or dinner.

Joints always appeal to men because they can know they can have several helpings. This one is distinguished by the fact that the meat will be cooked through but not dry and will have a lovely *jus*. We can't say it often enough, men just like the TEXTURE of meat, plain and simple (unless you've got a vegetarian, in which case he's probably repressing it). Maybe it goes back to men being the hunters, stoking up a bonfire on the savannah and roasting the prime cuts. Then bringing the scrag end home to the wives to make a casserole with, adding the veg they'd been gathering, of course.

As for pud, I started to make this when I found a recipe for apricot clafoutis in a French magazine at Marseilles airport. You can find a similar recipe in any good cookbook or on the internet. We were stranded there when our budget airline flight the night before was cancelled. I have often pondered since whether birds fly into the engines of more upmarket airlines too. Having nothing left to read at the end of the holiday I bought a mag largely to look at the pictures, my linguistic skills not being quite up to the text. Finally, a reason I wish I had paid more attention to my delightful French teacher, Madame Sloan. In consequence, I have never been certain that my translation of either the method or ingredients is entirely accurate. If anyone knows what '*tamisée*' means would they let me know.

To change gear. What do you think we are up to this time?

Menu 4 Any week day

Shepherd's pie with minted carrots	**Vampire rating 3** Before cooking the meat I always gently fry a large shallot, two chopped garlic cloves and a thinly sliced carrot. This gives a nice rich base to the dish. But, more than just the taste, there is the heavenly smell. I have, after many years, identified the source of that mouth-watering aroma I connect with French kitchens – it is cooked shallot! Eureka! I also add a generous squirt of tomato ketchup and a glug or six of red wine to the meat once it has browned. Many recipes might direct you to add beef stock, but personally, I would rather lubricate this sort of affair with wine.
Strawberries in lemon juice and sugar	Garnish with mint and vanilla ice cream.
Wine	Fleurie or other Beaujolais.
Ambiance	Madonna- but her '80's classics, or similar upbeat positive tracks.
Dress Code	Avoid long flowing skirts, kaftans and culottes (ghastly, please give yours to Oxfam). Surprise him with a sharp business suit. And, if you have long hair, why not wear it up à la Sarah Palin and Carla Bruni. No flats however posh. Always wear heels unless he is a midget.
Conversation	Ask him if his mummy used to make this dish. He is likely to open up about his childhood. Maintain eye contact and nod every so often in an empathetic manner. Everyone likes to talk about themselves.

	NEVER EVER MAKE A DEROGATORY REMARK ABOUT HIS MOTHER NO MATTER WHAT HORROR STORIES HE TELLS YOU. There will be plenty of time to fall out with her when you are married.

Music

It is time to change the pace a little.

Food

You are literally being the wolf in sheep's clothing this time.

The idea behind serving 'comfort' food in this dinner is to demonstrate that you can do 'homely' as well as more exotic fare. This will mark a transition from the MOD thinking of you as just an excellent cook to being a *potential homemaker*. Sneaky or what?

You are getting into the swing of this aren't you? We are being fairly gentle because we are assuming that you are on a learning curve at this point. If you have done a *cordon bleu* course / *Divertimenti* cookery class then bear with us a while longer.

Last one.

Menu 5 Saturday lunch

Stir fried salmon teriyaki with vegetables and noodles	**Vampire rating 1** Yes garlic – don't forget to throw it in! Your next question? Yes, you do need a wok. We have yet to meet a single person who does not have access to one. Ask your best friend to help you track one down.
Poached pear	With bought chocolate mousse.
Wine	Chablis, the ultimate Chardonnay

Ambiance	What about one of those compilations with tracks from a particular year? They are fun and will make him want to whisk you onto the dance floor. Ok, the kitchen floor. Try 1961 and 1963.
Dress Code	Frivolous and black – you should not wear anything light coloured in case it gets spattered with sauce. Accessorise with big beads. Tried glitter eye shadow?
Any other points?/Conversational gambits	Turn on Radio 4 in the kitchen and listen to Any Questions. He will think you are interested in current affairs. NB memorise the names of the PM and the presidents of at least 4 European countries. I used to try to learn these during lunch breaks at work with a good friend, Gabi. We claimed that Georges Rechs (fabulous dress designer) used to be the French president. She at least knew this was a joke.

Thinking man's crumpet

Caitlin, who I now realise is one canny married gal, admits that she does not usually have time to watch the news/read a paper but makes sure that she buys a newspaper on the day of a dinner party so that she does not come across as a complete nincompoop. This is an excellent idea since men, by a process of osmosis, manage to keep abreast of current affairs even if they work long hours. They do, don't they?! Unless they are knackered and just want a simpering creature by their side when they eat, they will appreciate it if you can engage them in suppertime conversation which is a bit more stretching than sweet nothings.

She also told me about a publication called *'the Week'* which apparently contains a succinct summary of world events for that week. Sounds like essential reading if the MOD is into Newsnight type programmes. Everyone needs at least one girlfriend who they can tap for useful information like this.

I keep a mental note of interesting snippets about current affairs that I come across in my travels which I can recycle or wheel out when watching University Challenge. Shall I give you an example? Well, a hunky banking friend sent me an enlightening e-mail explaining why the world's economy is heading south. He attributes it to the long-awaited downswing in the Kondratieff cycle (impressive or what!!). I can now opine knowledgably – OK- for at least 10 seconds - about the financial Armageddon. Attaching esoteric and, preferably Latin sounding, labels to events/syndromes always lends an air of gravitas and credibility to one's pronouncements I find. *Ipso facto!*

I also try and keep up with modern jargon. Recently, I learned that:

- You no longer suggest a 'window' for lunch/coffee but instead you ask someone whether they have time for an 'in transit' lunch/coffee. The automatic inference is that you are one busy lady.
- You do not refer to a group of people as having been made redundant. Rather they have been 'recalibrated' or 'right sized'.

Music
There should not be a reason to play the Beatles. They are the modern greats. So, you have now had five follow up meals each one showing a discernibly different music taste giving you the appearance of someone with eclectic and a broad church of experiences.

Food
Salmon? Isn't this a bit hackneyed? The sort of dish every mum tells their daughter to make on a first date? Probably, yes but in our capable hands this common old garden fish will be exciting. It is the technique of cooking it in this recipe which makes it special. It will be fabulous, compared to the ubiquitous dried-up salmon served up throughout the English summer by everyone and his wife. The flakes

are supposed to fall delicately apart and be pink, not white and glued together. Toss it on a wok and it should be light and delicious.

To follow we have chosen a mousse rather than an old favourite, a rum soufflé, which uses raw eggs. It is inadvisable to give uncooked eggs to pregnant women (are you?), the elderly, young children or prospective meal tickets for life. (We're not being mercenary but there is an element of truth in this.)

NB. For pears the fruit must be ripe but firm, a bit like your bum! We suspect a lot of people would urge you to waste tons of sugar when cooking pears. Ask yourself why? If the fruit is good then extra sweetening would be superfluous. If you can only get hard pears then go with the sugar though.

Now let's see where you should be at in the scoring stakes.

Not bad for a novice.

SCORE

1. *Commitment*	6	One notch above first base. This is the progress you want.
2. *Romance*	5	Probably too much garlic for him anyway and he's had a bad day at the office. Not important this time.
3. *Fun*	5	Feeling more at ease aren't you?

Achievement and expectations

Now you have gained confidence I think it is time to become a bit more adventurous. Shall we don our aprons again with a more specific purpose in mind and have some real fun? You are now ready to wield the ***stiletto in an oven glove. Courage mon brave!***

chapter 3

The lone soldier
How to deal with the unattached best friend

"It is a truth universally acknowledged that a single man in possession of a good fortune must be in want of a wife." Pride and Prejudice
Jane Austen (1775-1817) English author

Inspiration
Dorothy in *the Wizard of Oz*. More in manner than in looks please – red shoes and pig tails suit a certain kind of girl only. A cutesy look to belie your not-so-saccharine intentions.

But, we would add that your Dish could well have an unattached best mate who disagrees with Jane Austen about his friend's immediate future. Rest assured his ideas do not include matrimony.

The problem here is that the best friend is the lone soldier – you know the routine – he spouts drivel like *'he who travels fastest travels alone'*, *'a rolling stone gathers no moss'* etc. Needs to grow up. Preferably on a different continent.

Inevitably, his name will have been shortened to something like Josh. Recognise him? He possibly works in futures, plays the violin – would you believe to prove to himself/prospective short-term only girlfriends that he has a sensitive side and thinks all women will fall at his feet. He can whisk them to Gstaad for weekends so most of them do. If he wanted, he could be very well-spoken – went to a public school and all that jazz – but he is one of those guilt-afflicted types who prefers to affect a common touch so, except when he is inebriated, he has perfected an East End twang and speaks out of the corner of his mouth.

My husband *had* a best friend – note the use of the past tense please. They would go skiing to Aspen/zip to the Big Apple for long weekends (= 12 days) together with other unmarried, as opposed to unattached, males. I plead the Fifth Amendment on the subject of what became of this bosom chum but all I will say is that I first met him when he came to collect some keys. I misguidedly went to the trouble of making him and his on/off girlfriend homemade pâté naively believing that this welcoming gesture would win him over. Instead, I got 0/10. All it seemed to achieve was to signal that I was a HOMEMAKER /PB in waiting. Cue arrangements for the next boys' trip.

Learn from my howler.

The MOD is intelligent, of course, but will be as oblivious to his friend's animosity towards you as he is to your machinations. You will not get anywhere by whinging. BUT you will divorce or, at least, drive a wedge between Joshie Woshy and the Dishie Wishy by making it clear from the meal you serve that you know what he is up to and that you are not intimidated. More than this the message is that Josh's drinking buddy is moving on, even if he has not realised it quite yet.

As far as the MOD is concerned you will be performing your generous duties as an admirable hostess. How could he complain even if he picks up some of the mixed messages?

Here comes the plan

Before we discuss food let us pay special regard to the backdrop. This show is going to be uncharacteristically and unashamedly romantic. We warned you in the previous chapter against candlelight for intimate suppers *for two* since this is overtly amorous. Every rule has its exceptions (although *technically*, I suppose we are not advising that you break a rule since we are now going to be three, not two) and this is one meal where you *do* wish to convey the fact that two of those participating are starry-eyed about each other. We mean you and the MOD, *not* the MOD and Joshy.

So, put out the prettiest floral candles you can lay your hands on, perhaps even those scented ones that whiff like (pardon the expression but you know my drift) a tart's boudoir. These will send a clear message to the third party that, in the style of that steely role model, Lady Thatcher *'this lady's not for turning'* .

Why not rummage in the linen cupboard for the pale pink tablecloth and napkins your Aunt Jessica brought you back from Menorca a few years ago (isn't Aunt Jessie generous – this is actually the lacy cloth you bought last year in Sicily that you have not had the guts to show the MOD).

Pwitty Pink is going to be the *leit motif* (recurrent signature) of this event so carry the theme through into the food and drink. Do I need to say that there will not be any nibbles before dinner tonight. Nor a starter. Nor much in the way of carbohydrate. I do hope no one goes hungry. For tonight's performance the cook is going to be, and opine knowledgeably about how calorie and health conscious 'we' both are. This should not be difficult since this could be your specialist subject on *'Mastermind'*.

'Sweet Sue' Menu

Sea bass baked with ginger and spring onions with green beans and leeks and a tomato salad	Have soy sauce on the table. The salad should have a **Vampire rating 5** despite not having garlic. .
Fresh red and pink fruit salad with raspberry sorbet	No ice cream today!
Mint tea	Without sugar!
Drink	*'I am really not sure we feel like alcohol tonight. We had a heavy weekend and are thinking about not drinking on Wednesdays. Do you mind?'* You are not going to get away with this trick and of course Josh will come armed with a bottle. Economise and drink his.
Ambiance	Barry White or other love songs.
Dress code	Soft – now is the time for an ultra feminine tea dress.
Any other points?	Candles, flowers – the works.
Conversation	You will like this. What I call 'verbal incontinence'. Lots of 'we' this and 'we' that.

Music

We are not suggesting that you hold hands and have a smoochy slow dance with the MOD but just about everything else to create THAT ROMANTIC MOOD. Poor Josh.

Food

Josh will hardly be in a position to criticise you either since you have made such an elaborate meal. It actually sounds quite appetising doesn't it? If we were making it for someone we liked we would make it more substantial by offering saffron rice too. As this is not the case, you will have to have a filling snack before supper or afterwards with the Dish. You will not wish Him to retire starving. Perhaps you could prepare him a 'surprise' cheese plate which, *silly you*, you forgot to bring out at suppertime. A selection of excellent fresh goat's cheeses from the market and firm red grapes with bread sticks and oat cakes smeared with Aunt Jessica's onion marmalade would hit the spot.

Green beans and leeks
I adore leeks fried in butter and would normally say that this is how the vegetable ought to be prepared for maximum taste. Never mind. For a blander, more Spartan method, in tune with tonight's theme, you will be boiling both beans and the sliced leeks for a few minutes in the same pan. Provided they are not overcooked leeks should somehow retain a modicum of flavour.

Tomato salad
Slice some beef tomatoes and drizzle over some white wine vinegar and olive oil. Then chop up a small red onion and scatter the pieces on the top. Josh won't be pulling someone later with his breath reeking of this.

Fresh red and pink fruit salad with raspberry sorbet
Simply select some or all of the following chilled fruits: pitted cherries, blueberries, raspberries and strawberries. Spoon onto individual side plates or bowls, dust with icing sugar (you are unlikely to have a proper shaker but never fear – neither do I – all you need to do is to put a tbs of icing sugar in a sieve or tea strainer and shake) *and place a dollop of raspberry sorbet on the side. You will have some spare mint (see below) so garnish each bowl with a couple of sprigs.*

Mint tea
This will complement the dessert nicely. We said that there would come a time when you should surprise the MOD by making this and now would be just the ticket. Brew the tea in a decorative jug if

this looks more fetching than your teapot. Your guest is probably dying for some caffeine.

PS If he comes back for another round, might I suggest another light meal of roasted cod with wilted spinach and tomato stuffed with Arborio rice, basil and tomato. Oh – and roasted plums with a smattering of brown sugar and cinnamon for dessert.

Bet he heads for Pizza Hut.

PPS. I have relented and will tell you what became of 'my' 'Josh'. The last time I clapped eyes on him was nearly four years ago. He came for a rather splendid dinner and was so overcome by the domestic bliss of the scene that he was rendered quite speechless for the whole evening.

SCORE

1. *Commitment*	4	He has probably worked out you don't like Josh.
2. *Romance*	4	I think you'll have to take the initiative tonight.
3. *Fun*	8	You bet!

chapter 4

Befriending the wags

What should I do but drink away
The heat and troubles of the day?
Abraham Cowley (1618- 1667) English poet

Inspiration

Chardonnay in *Footballers Wives* or similar. These girls do not do skirts (minis only) or dresses except when they are going to a restaurant. So it's going to be Victoria Beckham's jeans if your budget can stretch to them (my favourite dress shop Zara is a good alternative for the financially challenged – or pick up Joseph jeans in the sales) or designer trackie bottoms – in white with a gold trim.

Meaning to be kind, Sarah has asked me to remind you that you should *only* do the latter IF your bottom is pert enough for white velour. All accessorised with vertiginous DKNY wedges. Mind your step though – I saw one of the 'mums' (that's how the mothers refer to each other!) topple over in a pair of these crossing a road when her little boy stumbled over them.

You've been out to supper with the MOD and some of his coupley friends a few times now. Of these, you have identified two women whom you might have befriended had you met them independently. Another two who are clearly the '*Alpha*' females in his circle. Guess which ones you are going to invite to lunch one Saturday when the menfolk are playing football, golf or bridge?

Well done. These women are important; after all, they have already reached the Promised Land. They are very powerful. Needless to say they will be telling their menfolk who is in and who is out. So it will be your chance to ingratiate yourself into their circle.

As we are talking woman-to-woman you will know the facts of life. It is more difficult to cultivate a female friend than one of the opposite sex who is amenable to flattery, fluttering eyelids and cleavage. Appealing to a man's baser instincts, whatever their age, is effective. Alas, our own kind present a harder, shrewder nut to crack. Like circling sharks we size each other up within nano seconds and ruthlessly edit out unacceptables. These are my principal conclusions about friendships amongst the fairer sex.

Warnings about women

1. It is difficult to make yourself popular if you are thin or very pretty.

2. Whatever sex you are, if you have a trust fund or what I call a 'product placement' surname you will always have lots of pals. In my time I have known three people whose surnames were synonymous with lots and lots of money and possibly a country pile or pad in Antibes somewhere along the line. They were comprised of a Carr (water biscuits), a Colman (mustard of course) and a Rothman (fags). All three were in gainful employment, delightful – and popular. They probably would have. been in demand had they been born into more ordinary stables. But, there was always the niggling doubt that people

were being that bit *nicer,* a tad *more deferential* to them than to little anonymous me.

At one point I toyed with the idea of advancing my theory about name recognition by adopting a new name such as McVitie and pretending that my grandfather founded the biscuit empire. What stopped me was the fear that I would be asked for the recipe for chocolate digestives.

As it happens I met my husband by latching onto a descendant of a very successful business family. Melanie, who was a super girl in her own right, a stunner, drank pints of water, had a fabulously clear complexion and was inundated with party invitations. Sometimes she graciously invited me to tag along. The crumbs from the captain's table were fun. Mel and I remained good chums after her wedding but lost touch when she started to produce heirs of her own. See 5 below. A pity.

If you are reading this for some reason Mel, thanks- and by the way you were right – Stephen *was* worth meeting although I did not think so when you took me to the party he was co-hosting. In retrospect it was perhaps short-sighted of me not to want to get to know him then because he was wearing a Father Christmas suit. But, at least he made a far more favourable impression when I re-met him at a hunt ball. Why don't you give me a call and we can catch up?

3.   Many of your single female friends will not be long-term friends. They are friends of convenience. Approach with caution particularly *if you catch them sniffing your boyfriend's aftershave.*

4.   I am sorry if I am the one to break the news that you

will be lucky to see for dust *any* girlfriends, however close you think you are, who get hitched way before you – even if you introduced them to their husband. And, if they have kids they might as well have moved to the moon since they may well have disappeared into the dull breast feeding, hairy armpit brigade they met at the NCT (National Childbirth Trust). Don't blame them for this because, if and when you have children, you'll see it's like getting sucked into an all-consuming vortex from which you emerge about 5 years later. Only then do you have time/energy to socialise again in the same (almost) carefree way. See 5.

5. It is all about symmetry. Come on. You know what I am driving at sweetie. It is no different to being recognisably the same as everyone else in your 'gang' when you were 10! See 6.

6. Women like cliques made up of *clones* in which we endlessly dissect the shortcomings of other women.

7. I am sure you will wonder if it is better to meet the WAGS at a restaurant but inviting them home gives you a golden opportunity to establish your credentials. Entertaining is a disarming tactic which will put them at ease and represents your best chance of gaining access to the pack. By all means when you are IN, arrange to rendezvous at the fitness centre.

So, let's take a closer look at the other halves, shall we? The trick here is to fit in. In order that you are accepted as a kindred spirit you should buy some women's magazines to research which food fads are in vogue. I have an idea that Atkins may be *passé*. Then you will be armed for your solicitous text messages to your guests to enquire if there is anything they do not eat. These sorts of women are far too busy to speak to anyone on the phone but they are in constant, laborious electronic communication with each other. You will have to get up to speed with the latest technology.

We are pretty certain that at least one of them will text you to say that she subscribes to the 'ht dit' (= 'hot diet' fad of the moment). Another one is bound to only eat 'macro' (= macrobiotic food?') or 'gltn fre' (=gluten free). I would not blame you if you felt an irresistible urge to compete by feigning some obscure 'fd algy' (= food allergy) yourself!

Ingredients

For this precious, sorry I meant, ecologically and carbon footprint conscious crew, it is vital that all ingredients that you buy are organic, Fair Trade, low fat and low calorie. Saying, "It's low-fat!" brightly, as you bring a dish to the table, will gladden these girls' hearts. They're secretly grateful (so long as there's a calorie-laden pud), as it means the blow-out is at least contained. A man's heart, on the other hand, will drop, along with his ardour.

Make sure that you let slip where you shop too. Our suspicion is that they will strongly favour those companies that deliver organic produce to your door or the smaller retailers over supermarkets, except of course for the big new *Waitrose* which has opened up by the roundabout which is so fantastically convenient for the school run, isn't it?

Remember, at the end of lunch to inform them of the exact GI content of their meal. Then, open a box of luxury, hand made, full cream, Belgian chocolates which 'Aunt Jessica' gave you yesterday. Watch them disappear.

Hot drinks

None of them is going to admit to drinking caffeine – so regular tea and even decaffeinated coffee will be off limits. You must stock up with an extensive range of herbal teas. I gather from one chic neighbour, Sasha, who can be relied upon to know exactly what is *au courant* in any material sphere, be it hot drinks (see below), holiday destinations (Portugal, Dubai, South Coast), furniture or furnishings, that the *cognoscenti* like Chinese Sencha Green Tea with Natural Lemon.

Incidentally, it is an idea to keep a couple of sachets in your handbag for you to produce when you are out and about. This human barometer of good taste whipped out her sencha when she popped in one morning since I obviously have such appalling taste that anything in my cupboard was bound to be undrinkable to anyone with a more discerning palate. Quite possibly true. I have belatedly cleansed my house of PG Tips and bought a container load of *Sencha* (can anyone tell me what on earth this is?) from Waitrose.

I am not sure I should mention this but Sarah has started to bring her own tea bags over here too. Hers is a caffeine-free variety called Rooibosch. Sarah admits to an insufferably holier-than-thou approach to giving up caffeine. She won't live longer, it will just seem like it

Cold drinks

You may find it prudent to have several chilled bottles of wine on hand. It will readily become apparent that your acquaintances know as much about wine as you did a few weeks ago; they will glug anything which is alcoholic, chilled and white. Your newly discovered knowledge of grape varieties would be wasted on this bunch so you may as well plump for any inexpensive 'crap' New World white. I use this term in a flip way since they will all be eminently drinkable. What's more - as I am no wine connoisseur - sweet, chilled cheap whites would be divine to me. The hubby and my friend Timothy both of whom are genuine bacchanalian experts watch with horror when I dilute a glass of claret (north of £40 a bottle) with Perrier to make a rather delicious spritzer.

Come to think of it, apart from getting rid of his precious trouser press, my only other matrimonial transgression that Stephen knows about – so far- is when I opened a bottle of this pricey stuff for a home-made pizza meal with Timothy. Apparently I was supposed to go for the *Valpolicella* on the other side of the room. Whoopsie.

Better put several bottles of supermarket still water in the fridge as well. I don't know why but quite a few women don't do bubbles in water but they knock back lager, champagne and good old G&T. Serve with a slice of Fairtrade lime if such a thing exists; pretty.

Menus

We deal with food after drink on this occasion to reflect the order of importance to the wives and girlfriends.

Choose from the following selection of light lunches which are all appropriate for three women watching their waist lines. Bread, as a carbohydrate, is a no no.

Puy lentils with grilled skinless and boneless cod and spinach	**Vampire rating 2** Perfect in winter. Unobjectionable. Ladle balsamic over the lentils so they have a decent flavour. Sounds healthy and with luck they'll ask you for the recipe. The ultimate compliment.
Monkfish with tomatoes stuffed with rice, basil and garlic served on a bed of round lettuce	**Vampire rating 3** A slimline meal for someone who has told you they are dieting to get into a dress at the weekend. This will show how considerate a person you are.
Salad nicoise	Use fresh tuna not John West tinned (save this to have with salad cream and sweet corn on rye bread for when you are eating by yourself).

Black olives can be a disaster, too hard and resembling goats' droppings. There are two |

	rules with salad olives – never buy pitted varieties and always choose plump oily olives which do not come in a jar or tin. Tinned or jars are ok for cooking with but you need ones which are more forceful in flavour if they are to be eaten neat. M&S olives would fit the bill nicely. Normally they would get a ham salad so this will be considerably nicer.
Smoked salmon with marinated finely sliced fennel and dill.	Fabulous low-carb meal, you'll win friends. This is nothing short of sensational. A great brunch dish too – see Chapter 9. Soak sliced fennel (sprinkled over with lemon to prevent discolouration) overnight in a marinade comprised of sugar dissolved over a gentle heat in water and white wine vinegar. To assemble, pile the fennel on plates and drizzle over some oil into which you have stirred some torn dill. Place the salmon on top and scatter over some more of the herb.
Chicken Caesar Salad	**Vampire rating 2** I am afraid that the mob will associate dried up shreds of chicken in this salad with dire golf club fare. Only make this with moist cooked roast chicken. Hand round the croutons separately – dreaded bread!
Avocado, beef tomato and mozzarella stack with a pesto sauce	**Vampire rating 4** Good for a summery day.

Good quality shop bought quiches with a mixed leaf salad	Quiche is good to serve to someone who has a hearty appetite or an energetic morning playing tennis or spending their husband's money. As a CookSmart devotee it is obvious to buy quiche. Pep it up with an interesting salad.
Feta cheese, water-cress and spinach salad with grapefruit and orange segments	Women who like to think of themselves as sophisticated would love this sort of salad.
Asparagus with poached egg and Parma ham	Different.
Cold chicken with baked potato and crunchy green beans and ratatouille	For the one woman in the group you actually like.
Ambiance	Oasis or U2. Will Young, James Blunt? Uncontroversial, reasonably modern background wallpaper. The key is not to be pretentious.
Dress code	See above. Nothing which might arouse envy.
Any other points?	Display ostentatiously any invitations to events which the girls might want to go to themselves- Henley, royal garden parties, restaurant openings etc. They will think you mix in the right circles and want a piece of the action. Plus a photograph of the two of you somewhere exotic, but not in a swimsuit showing off your figure.

Safe topics of conversation

This subject is way too important to confine to a box. You need to keep your conversation innocuous.

Limit chat to one or more of the following areas which these women expect you to talk about:

- exotic holidays
- aerobics classes
- clothes, hair
- second homes
- Daniel Craig
- Daniel Craig – he's worth mentioning twice

Oh, and how could I forget – Tubes. I do not understand why but you will find that women of a certain ilk who barely know you will be telling you all about their 'fertility issues'. I have learned more about IVF from virtual strangers than from any programme by Lord Winston.

I use the word conversation in this context loosely since your role is to flatter and smile, certainly not to correct silly mistakes such as the one made by a friend of ours who pronounced *foie gras* 'foy grasse.'

Resist the temptation to mock idiosyncrasies too. I am not very good at this. Having dinner at *Nobu* one evening with several of my husband's financier friends and their standard-issue giraffe girlfriends, I unthinkingly asked one of these women, Kelly, who was chain smoking, how cigarettes fitted in with her '*Planet Organic*' lifestyle. She was not amused and I suppose it is not entirely surprising that our friendship did not blossom.

Sarah's advice on safe topics of conversation is that you don't know these women well, they're not your friends, so don't spill your guts. Don't tell them anything confessional or sensitive ie your boyfriend's fetishes or that you are swingers. Stick to safe, neutral subjects, which are also fun ie bitching about celebrities, who's lost or gained weight/had surgery. You can't go wrong with school runs, property values. Sometimes she finds it wins friends to complain about her lack of resolve in the gym, inability to resist cream cakes/chocolate/anything with calories in. It makes you seem more human and less of a threat – as you are obviously not superwoman with iron resolve and limitless willpower.

Petty, unthinking snobberies will have to be endured as well. Two women I know illustrate what I mean. They are both hitched to successful city men and have a second home abroad. Only when asked about their place they have both retorted '*it's not a house/apartment, it's a villa*'.* I suppose a villa sounds like it's a more substantial edifice than a mere house, sort of one step beneath a castle. One of them '*sleeps 10*'. I like the extra level of superfluous detail volunteered. Personally I would settle for a shack anywhere in the Med... Cassis, St. Tropez, Mougins. Magical. Any will do.

When we were talking about this place the other day Sarah called it MOUGINS with a hard 'g' as in 'smug git'. I think it should be pronounced with a soft 'j' sound, as in 'jealous'.

In similar vein I learned from Jess, who has acquired a 'bolt hole' (this is a trendy name for a second home within commuting distance of your first home) that a relative of Gordon Brown's wife *possibly* owns the house next door! My guess is that it is a perfectly nice, ordinary bloke with no celebrity connections whatsoever. I am hoping to spend a few days at Jess's place next Easter with the kids and will be making some enquiries about the locals. But, if Gordon starts to make some irrational or imprudent decisions in the spring, show some understanding please since it could be that he has spent a weekend from hell in the country next to some unreasonably noisy neighbours.

Hungry? When they have staggered out, treat yourself to a Snickers bar.

* According to my husband's 1970 Collins New (huh!) English Dictionary a villa is '*a country seat*' or '*a suburban residence*'. A house is only '*a building intended for human habitation*'.

SCORE

1. Commitment   7   Yes, the message will get back to him.

2. Romance   0   Err, no.

3. Fun   5   You had fun but they were largely ghastly.

chapter 5

Being Florence Nightingale
Tending to the invalid

"Nous avons sur les bras un homme malade- un homme gravement malade"
'We have on our hands a very sick man!'
Nicholas 1 of Russia (1796-1855)

Inspiration

It is a touch Oedipal – surrendering to a woman in *loco parentis*. But all men like to flirt with an attractive nurse. Think of coquettish Barbara Windsor in her heyday. You are going to become an updated Florence Nightingale minus the lamp. Watch *Holby City*, *Casaulty*, *ER* and *Carry On* films for ideas. You need to perfect a concerned furrow in your brow. Something to practice in front of the mirror of the loo at the office.

Wearing a fancy dress nurse's uniform is too obvious. If it is summer you could go for a crisp white dress I suppose. This is the only time in this epicurean journey that we will be recommending that you wear flat shoes. White and preferably deck shoes. Not trainers – they are too bulky.

Illness does strange things to men. In certain limited circumstances it can bring out their finest qualities. This is because the neediness in question impacts on a man's capabilities rather than to his fragile emotional side. In *extremis,* if a girlfriend is incapacitated or in genuine pain a certain kind of helplessness can appeal. Think of Carey Grant in *An Affair to Remember.* The key points to remember here are:

- There must be absolutely no histrionics.
- Nor a red and runny nose.
- If you have got an STD it is probably best to keep him well away!

Ashley, an eligible bachelor I knew was transformed into a model of chivalry in less time than it takes to yell 'Avalanche!' when his new girlfriend, Susie, a novice skier, fell awkwardly on the slopes fracturing her fibula or was it tibia? He instantly assumed complete charge of her repatriation and ministered to her like a bird with a broken wing. Sweet. They are now married with two 'high spirited' boys.

Alas, the same transformation does not happen when men fall prey to ill health.

Shortly after I met my dearest one he was admitted to hospital with a hernia. Although I was new on the scene he clearly revelled in the fact that he could tell mum and his best friend that he had someone to look after him. The *privilege* of collecting him, his bag, bouquets from his sisters and the world's heaviest fruit basket (from Harrods), a gift from his mother, was accorded to me. Somehow I managed to leave mum's largess in the taxi. She does not know to this day. No doubt she would have thought this was a deliberate attempt to elbow her aside. Maybe subconsciously it was but I swear I just had my hands full.

When I had finally got this lot back to his place I cooked, cleaned and shopped for a week solidly while he convalesced. I even took time off work. Mug. As soon as he could limp he and his mates were off partying. He took a pretty little thing from some American bank I recall. If I had my time again I would have just dumped him at home with the cleaning lady and given him a flyer from the local Chinese.

Now you have read my cautionary tale you will know the answer to the following question. When the Dish is bedridden what is the correct response if you are not living together? Is it (a) buy a wicker basket, line it with a red checked tea towel and fill it with savoury pies, lasagne and pastries and a hand painted mug with flowers (b) leave him to get better – he is not your responsibility or (c) head to Marks?

The correct answer is of course (c). *Multum in parvo* – much in little.

If you are not living with the MOD do not behave like his mother. Let her rush around and cluck over him like a hen. Think what a sophisticated city girl would do. Answer – text him on the hour to find out what his temperature is – you can say you are monitoring his progress in case he needs to be rushed to A&E - and head to the supermarket. This is the time to buy the ready-made soup, the tins of baked beans and grapes. These items will show that you care - but at a respectable distance.

Where you score points will be on extras. Make a toddy from hot water, squeezed lemon juice, a teaspoon of honey and whisky (unless he's on medication – a coma would present difficulties). Don't bother with measures – he is not driving anywhere so you can afford to be generous with booze. Alternatively, try out hot lemon spiked with amaretto. The poor lamb is *desperately* ill so let him drink from a mug for once.

If alcohol makes him nauseous (that's a new one) you will have to make a teetotal drink. The old fashioned favourites are a bit unexciting but will do the job. Go for hot water with a couple of teaspoons of commercial raspberry jam (my late Russian born grandmother made this *molyneux* with her excellent home made conserve) or hot water with a squeeze of lemon juice and a teaspoon of honey. OJ may have to be endured.

If you are *in situ* (i.e. you live with him, ignorami!) the *modus operandi*, (ie the way you proceed, ditto) apart from drinks that is, must be quite different. This is the time for subliminal messaging. Men like to be cosseted when they are unwell so this is the perfect chance to show your feminine softer side, whilst not undermining your credibility. Don't be at his beck and call, but it's show time! Bring on the Florence Nightingale routine.

How do you do this? Prepare a range of comforting and nutritious nursery food which can slip down a painful throat.

Male readers will violently disagree, but dear reader, take it from one who knows, the male of the species makes a meal of being unwell. As if on cue, my efforts this evening (a Thursday) have just been interrupted by a call from a delightful family friend who let me know that he was at last getting over a bad cold caught from some friends last weekend. He had had '*a basin full*' but reassured me that he was '*over the worst*' and I need not worry. I assure you I was in no danger of panicking. This was a sniffle we were talking about, not pneumonia!

Many men are frustrated doctors. The internet has become a cornucopia of scare stories/information about your *diseases*. I heard someone say that some people who all but faint at the sight of blood are unable to take up medicine as a career, so they like to do the next best thing – become a patient. Accordingly, they will want to be mollycoddled by mum, matron or nanny. This is therefore probably one of the rare occasions in which the Dish will not notice that you are exhibiting PB tendencies. Accordingly, this is the perfect time to make him a proper pud. Rice pudding is ideal food for someone who is ill but it has too overly cosy wosy connotations for you to make this at other times.

Here is a selection of perfect foods for the injured soldier.

Fried eggy bread	Cut into soldiers.
Soft boiled eggs or poached egg on toast	Granary bread makes the best toast.
Baked beans on toast	Ladle on the butter.
Superior scrambled eggs	Use a bain marie, butter not marg and cream or crème fraiche, not milk
Tomatoes fried in lots of butter, seasoned and served on buttered brown toast	Use ripe toms or not at all.
Jacket potato with lashings of butter, grated extra mature cheddar cheese and lightly boiled broccoli florets	Make sure the shell is crispy – you need a hot oven. Limp potatoes will get you no thanks.
Superior fish pie	**Vampire rating 2** *"Cheese – 'milk's leap towards immortality'"* Clifton Fadiman (1904-1999) American author Cheddar cheese needs to be of the extra mature variety whenever you need it for a recipe. Soapy cheese is soapy. Two things will differentiate your pie from the traditional version. First, add garlic to the butter before you mix in the flour for the *roux* to make your sauce. This lends a subtle depth of flavour. Second, poach the fish in milk and water which has already been simmered for at least 10 minutes with a sliced shallot and black pepper. No need to bother with greens since you can pop in the odd pea anyway.

the dish

Ambiance	Shh – he's got a headache.
Dress code	You are nanny, mummy, staff nurse. You need to look as if you are in charge. White dress as aforementioned, work suits ok, tailored dress ok, tailored trousers ok.
Any other points?	Get as many Bond films as you can on DVD. Watch *Casino Royale* yourself (several times).
Conversation	Brief and to the point. You are 'on duty'.

Music
As he has regressed to childhood we were half thinking about a sing along. In reality he is likely to be prone in front of the TV so music is not required. My husband has some Buddhist chants that he swears by when he has a migraine.

Desserts
His mother used to make him nice sweets when he was little. Ahh. Why don't you too?

Bought treacle tart or tarte tatin	Serve with vanilla ice cream.
Rice pudding	How about a nice dollop of jam?
Lightly stewed interesting fruit – peaches, plums mixed with apple, cherries or strawberries	Tread carefully. But, if you know He is a rhubarb man then stew some with a dash of lemon juice, OJ, some cinnamon and sugar.
Buy some confectionary – boiled sweets, jelly babies etc	Under 5's childhood favourites are best.

Rice pudding

He is verging on whiny so we are going to give you a hand on this one and spell out how to make it.

An easy method of preparing this dessert is to take a regular sized heatproof ramekin dish. Put in 2 tbsp of short grain (pudding) rice, 2 tsps of sugar and then fill the dish up to ¾ inch below the rim with milk. Place in a pre-heated oven at a setting of 180 degrees for 40-45 mins. If you slightly overcook the rice do not panic – this can be corrected by adding a few drops of milk.

I always place the ramekin on a small baking dish because invariably the milk boils over and it is a bore to have to scrub the oven to remove dried burnt milk. If the pudding passes muster the theme can be varied by adding some sultanas and/or cinnamon before going in the oven.

Comments

The *mise en scène* is particularly important when you are playing at being nursie. Making the patient feel comfortable and looked after should be your main concerns. So, for once let him eat in bed. If you can, lug the TV into the bedroom so he can watch re-runs of Top Gear *ad nauseam*. There is nothing quite so irritating as crumbs in bed so buy a tray with folding legs and put out a couple of napkins.

SCORE

1. *Commitment*	8	He now needs you.
2. *Romance*	0	You will have to sort yourself out tonight.
3. *Fun*	2	Grit your teeth. You are after the ring.

chapter 6

Avoiding confrontation
Being the perfect step-mother

"And I'd never wear such a fashionable gown that you couldn't climb on my lap whenever the fit took you"
Fanny Fern (1811-1872) American columnist/novelist

Inspiration

Julie Andrews as Maria in *the Sound of Music or Mary Poppins*. Learn some songs from the DVD and effect a permanent, cheerful demeanour. Go to the hygienist and have your teeth cleaned professionally so they are dazzlingly white for that 24/7 'mummy' smile. Avoid clothes that are dry cleanable only. If the kids are small dig out something pink and frilly from the closet and you will automatically be deemed to have immaculate taste.

I endorse Mary Poppins' maxim *'A spoonful of sugar helps the medicine go down'*. I think it will be *only* after the third month that the bombshell is dropped. He mentions, almost *sotto voce*, that he has some children. Four in fact. Two older children from his first marriage and two tiny tots from his second. Two ex-wives and three mortgages. Lots of statistics for you to digest here. But then, he is an accountant.

This is a wonderful opportunity to demonstrate your (hitherto non-existent) maternal qualities. To show the MOD that – despite the fact that (a) you are childless (b) you have no experience of children and (c) you said on the first date that you couldn't stand little people – you have step-mother potential.

But happy children are not hungry children. Is it just a matter of shipping in oven ready pizza, chips and fish fingers (Sarah and I love them)? NO. NO. NO. What's wrong with you? He'll think you are going to turn them into obese dysfunctional slobs. They probably will not live with him (thank your lucky stars) and he is unlikely to quiz his ex-wife about their daily meals but believe me, when they are in your charge he will expect you to do right by them or you will be back on the single scene quicker than you can say *'Charlie and Lola'*.

I am not saying you should become their nutritional guardian – this is not your role. By all means procure industrial quantities of fizzy drinks from Costco – coke (not Diet) and Pepsi, Fanta, Lemonade, 7 Up, Iron Bru and whatever else you can get your hands on. Not alcopops.

All children adore sweets. Lay in truckloads of them. This is a sweetener. Literally. What of it? Bribery works. One girlfriend of mine who was unused to handling children asked me what she should do if she found herself alone in the car outside the shops with the putative step children refusing to get out. Tempting as it is, social services and the police would have something to say if she just did a runner. I said stuff them with crisps and sweets. I did not hear her complain again.

But the key to having sweet natured children for longer than it takes to devour a packet of revels (3 mins 24.5 secs) is activity. You need to overcome their natural suspicion (*litotes = mega understatement*) of the OTHER woman plus the usual boredom. Thus, food preparation is a heaven sent task to occupy their little noddles.

Easy. Let's divvy up the kids between the older ones – they may be only 10 and 14 (hang on, He's only 32 so how old was he when the oldest one was born? He can't be 14 – more like 12) – and the small ones – 4 and 7.

I learned what to do the hard way, since before I had children, I had never clapped eyes on any of this odd species of human. It was a bit of a shock then to be confronted with two of my friend's small children, Anton and Ariadne, shortly after I met Stephen. They are nice enough as children go but since they are corralled into spending every spare minute of their leisure time with pursuits I find too tedious (violin, cello – yawn – *more* violin, cello and orchestra practice) I did not have much to say to them or *vice versa*.

Daunting too, since a previous attempt to entertain *one* of Stephen's nieces was unexpectedly hard work. *Two* children were going to be exhausting. Carmen was taken (a) for a walk (b) for a trip to the puppet theatre and (c) to McDonald's. Curiously, during the eight hours she was with us she did not go to the loo once. Perhaps she knew we were nervous about having to take her to a bathroom. This was a tiring day enlivened only by the fact that my husband discovered that a man holding a pretty little girl's hand will have strangers smile and say hello to him. Not dissimilar to taking a dog for a walk.

Good advice for an unattached male looking for an unusual pulling strategy. Not so good for a woman, since there is precious little collegiality amongst mums who can be fed up with children and oblivious to the sight of a child in a pram. We notice things like what the pram pusher is wearing. A few seasons ago it was crocs. I am not a fan myself since street dirt permeates the holes leaving your feet looking as if you have contracted an awful skin disorder.

Anyway, back to the other kids. I had devised a new and brilliant strategy. When they arrived for tea I ushered them into our old sub-basement kitchen and put them to work making revolting green 'Scooby Doo' fairy cakes. They had an amazing time and possibly thought I actually liked them.

Grumpy older children

As soon as the introductions are over we would suggest you whisk the youngsters towards the kitchen to *join you in making* (a more grown up term than mere 'help'- the theory being that by addressing them in an adult manner they will behave in a mature fashion too) one of the following foods which they might actually find exciting:

Sushi	Wow – this is exotic! And way cheaper than eating sushi out. We doubt they have made this before. You haven't either, but improvise. They probably think a California roll is either a kind of soft bap or a rap star.
Home made pizzas	Another economy winner! Mum may have bought them a packet of dough mix once but with you they will be making the real McCoy and they can choose their own toppings.
Home made lamb burgers	Let the kids mix the ingredients for these – they can be mini versions of the ones you make the lads in Chapter 12 or turn them into meatballs by baking them in the oven for 15 mins and then cooking them further in a sauce made of passata, fried onion and fried garlic. Serve with spaghetti.
Pasta with pesto sauce	Why not let the children have a go with a pestle and mortar for this sauce? Yes, you'll have to buy one.

Ice creams	Your raspberry parfait might be a tad sophisticated but the honeycomb will be right up their street. They can break up the honeycomb and do any mixing that does not involve electrics.
Ice lollies	Allow them to choose a fruit juice to freeze in those fabulous plastic ice lolly containers – the ones which come with incorporated sticks. (You can buy them at Sainsbury's) They can pour them into the lolly holders.
Cake	Hmm – look, the Dish is going to leave you to it this afternoon, to see if you sink or swim, so it's ok to indulge in some quiet PB (plum bottling) to ingratiate yourself with the children. How about making a seriously chocolaty cake?
Ambiance	For the older ones - they will be difficult, so let them choose a funky radio station such as Kiss FM. This is the perfect compromise as you won't have to keep up with what is hip. Warn the neighbours if you live in a flat.
Conversation	My mother, who was a teacher, would advise you to speak softly and never raise your voice. To this day I find this sibilant approach makes me want to SCREAM! My own view is that picking the right questions is vital. I find that asking a child what school it attends, what its favourite subject is and who they like will elicit very detailed answers. Small children are also parrots, so if you are imaginative you can find out all sorts of things about mum.

Sushi
To make the sushi (there will be no raw fish if you wish to avoid the mother giving the MOD grief on the phone later) you will need the following.

Rolls of sushi wrap	Obtainable from the supermarket.
Cooked ordinary rice	I found on the one occasion I made this with sticky rice it was impossible to work with.
Avocado pear	
Cucumber, tomato	If a daughter is feigning anorexia she can nibble on these until she succumbs to the other eats.
The usual suspects	Soy sauce, wasabi paste, pickled ginger, cooked salmon, cooked tuna, smoked salmon.

Put all the ingredients in bowls for the children to help themselves to and have smaller bowls (you could use egg cups or ramekins) to dunk the sushi into soy sauce. Set to work on a large work surface or the kitchen table creating combinations of the above ingredients and making them into sushi rolls. If you have any chop sticks these will be more fun to use as implements than spoons.

Cheese pizza – a clear winner
I worked out that this is a child's top fantasy food when I asked Hayley's five year old what grub she liked best and she replied *'choize pizza'*. Judging by her mother's apparent lack of interest in the kitchen I wonder if this was the only nourishment that the little thing was given.

I was also asked to give a friend's sophisticated ten-year-old daughter a lift home and I took the opportunity to quiz her on what she thinks about food too. She is rake thin and said, not surprisingly, that she likes grilled fish. I would guess her mother drills her to say that this is her favourite food. But, things picked up and I suspect we were getting closer to the truth when she added enthusiastically that she *really* likes cheese pizza and loves, but does not particularly like, her brother. I knew it!

Check to see whether your oven has a proving facility. Like me you may have one without realising it. I had not looked at the instructions for my Neff oven (I cannot bring myself to read excruciatingly turgid things like sheet music, legal cases about tree root subsidence or overflowing loos and any kind of instruction manual) and it took a tiny tot to draw my attention to the panel above the oven with a small picture of a loaf pan filled with dough.

Cake making – a recipe for disaster?
Ask a child to grease, then line a cake tin. If you don't have one use some paper fairy cake cases. The children can mix up all the ingredients for as long as they like in a large bowl (you will be adding hot ingredients). Then the mixture can be transferred to the tin or spooned into the cases.

Be warned! If they are prone to squabbling you will need two of everything – bowls, spoons etc.

The little ones

Aren't they cute – when they are asleep perhaps. Have you found on occasions such as this that you are stumped when visiting children ask if you have any 'proper' toys? Disappointingly, I have found that most of them do this in either a whiny or peremptory manner, as if you are the hired help. For boys, who can be so spoilt, this probably means something expensive. I confess to coveting one super boy's miniature Batmobile specially imported from China. It is not entirely surprising in this part of town that, when I heard a group of children being asked to make a resolution for the next year, one of them replied '*I am going to try to be nicer to my nanny*'.

A few minutes into a playdate with one four year old chappie, Rex, I found that the honest answer I was obliged to give him to a version of the standard request was – no. The DVD collection was not macho enough and it was raining so the garden was out. Thankfully, he leapt at the chance of making gingerbread biscuits. And, in fact Rex was having such a good time that he refused to go home with his mother when she came to collect him. That was ok by me since he is a lovely child and very well mannered plus my daughter has set her cap at him. A smart cookie my girl – his parents live in a 'palazzo' in a premier central London address along with Masserati loads of the super-rich, ambassadors and diplomats. Now that I am in the know about architectural terminology I would not dream of calling it a house.

To business – children under 8 have an innate and inexplicable love of messy pastimes such as decorating cakes and biscuits with sprinkles. They also like to think they are helping you create something wonderful for Daddy to eat.

You will be taking the lead with this age group rather than offering alternatives. This is what you need to engage their interest.

Have wipes and a towel on standby for disgustingly sticky hands *and* feet. Small children are oblivious to the amount of ingredients they knock onto the floor during cooking and they always tread in it.

Gingerbread men	These are wonderful to make ; gooey, messy and you can cut shapes with a cutter! Hooray!!
Sickly sweet cake	Lots and lots of mixing. Then more still.
A salad for daddy	With fields full of peas/broad beans and mixing up of vinaigrette. Do not expect this to be edible.
Mini pizzas	(as above) Interminable rolling out is an excellent time killer.

Any other life saving points?	Yes - and this never fails – ask them to help you put out some crisps/Pringles for Daddy. They won't make it to the table.
Ambiance	For the little ones any fun dance music you like. Toploader 'Dancing in the Moonlight', 'Take That', Gnarls Barkley (wrote Crazy - the best selling single a while back). You will be encouraging them to take to the floor with you and the background noise will help keep you sane while they scream their heads off. Make sure you have a tinny nursery rhyme compilation. You will find yourself listening to Ba Ba Blacksheep at least a dozen times. Sorry if you live in Notting Hill, this is probably banned now.
Conversation	Guarded. They are old enough and smart enough to know that mum will expect them to relay any clangers.

Achievement and expectations

Right, that was not so difficult. But, do not forget that children tend to have a mother or two lurking in the background. They may not be quite as delighted with you after their *repas chez toi*. What do you think we are going to do to, *I mean*, for her?

SCORE

1. *Commitment* 8 A big hurdle crossed.

2. *Romance* 4 He is on for it as he is relieved. You are too knackered.

3. *Fun* 5 Much better than you expected.

67

chapter 7

All's fair in love and war
Ex-girlfriends
and ex-spouses

"Armed neutrality" – *Message to Congress 1917*
Thomas Woodrow Wilson, (1913-1921)
28th President of the United States

Inspiration

Study closely Betty Davis in *All about Eve*. As she says in the film *'Fasten your seatbelts, it's going to be a bumpy ride!'*

It had to happen sooner or later and now it has. The Dish is wheeling out a former girlfriend who just happens to be his former long term sweetheart – believe me, they all have one. Inevitably, She will have shortened her name to Charlie/Plum/Tuppy to effect intimacy.

You *must* action my plan if the ex does any ONE of the following things:

•   texts or calls the MOD's mobile every day.

- e-mails him at work more than once a week (difficult to prove).
- phones home but does not leave a message. Do 1471.
- hangs up when you answer. Do 1471.
- invites him to drinks/lunch/theatre without you.
- works in fashion and wants to introduce him to some lonely Russian models she has befriended. You would have to be a confident lass to let your beloved go clubbing with high-cheekboned fashion babes with PhDs in nuclear physics!

One of my husband's former beloveds, Katherine, was *from the valleys, boyo*. For years when he even mentioned her name – *Catheeerin*- he did so in an irritating, slightly breathy, hushed tone. I found some faded pictures of this paragon in a cupboard while cleaning and they clearly did not do her charms justice. My guess is she must have been rather lovely to have made such a deep rooted impact on his psyche. Significantly, one of the reasons he put her on a pedestal was that they would often cook together of an evening. I can picture the cosy domestic scene now, stirring their supper pot. Even now he speaks gently when he recalls that she prepared her delicious signature dish on special occasions – something I had never heard of called 'chicken *tonnato*'. Hilarious! Boiled chicken with a tinned tuna and anchovy sauce. Sounds delicious. I wonder why they did not marry?

Incidentally, the tactic we're going to employ also goes for "the one that got away" i.e. a woman friend he's always fancied/fantasised about but never went out with. She's remained a (single) friend, and fancies him too, in a predatory way. She will be fake nice-as-pie to you, but with an edge. She wants you out of the way, but we're too clever for that.

Now, your Charlie has apparently just landed a Terribly Busy and Important Job that makes *you* feel like a 'non-status *fraulein*', but has e-mailed Him *at the office* (= she clearly did not want to run the risk of your deleting a message sent to you at his blueyonder address at home) to say that she will manage to drop by for a bite to eat on Thursday evening about 6.30. Is that OK? This is tantamount to a declaration of war.

Presumptuous too. Maybe she doesn't know you're living with him now – or very nearly – to give her the benefit of the doubt. But he's agreed without consulting you so she obviously has retained some residual hold over your beloved. Interesting.

Although you have not met her, you are pretty much certain that it is her photo you found at the back of his top right desk drawer (after you had deposited the entire contents on the floor to see what you could find). She was posing, *would you believe it*, on the terrace of the *same* hotel he took you to in Positano (the *Poseidon – in my humble opinion* much more romantic and chic than the *Sireneuse* where lots of the well heeled British congregate), clad in a confident green *Melissa Oderbash* bikini (or similar chic/sexy/hip number), exposing rather too much broiled pink skin for your liking. How long ago this was is difficult to establish from the blurred date stamp on the back. Intriguingly, he has written in manuscript something I was told by an ex about his perfect former girlfriend *'you know you are with the right person when two and two makes five!'* For someone who crunches numbers for a living this is a rather disturbing comment.

How charming, there are no hard feelings. I stopped believing in fairies, Father Christmas and winning the lottery a long time ago. Men at least have the decency to be upfront when they regard you as superfluous; women are more adept at concealing their agenda. You and I know exactly what this little *'kitten woman's'* game is, don't we?

Here's the plan

Contrary to those negative views you may hold about the wisdom of entertaining an ex – wife or girlfriend, we adhere firmly to the view that this is actually something to encourage. Once. On your own territory. It will really be quite the most unsettling experience for *Charlotte* when the person she expects to be hostile *appears* to be terribly nice. You are to deploy a turbo powered version of the tactic we used to repel the unattached male.

By the way, I managed to see off an ex of hubby's from the Southern Hemisphere, who popped up in town with a new job, by suggesting to him that, instead of the two of them having an intimate catch-up lunch in the city, that she came round to meet the family. Byee to her too.

Sarah agrees entirely that you have to be super-nice to the ex girlfriend. If you snarl, you'll look like a bitch. She'll know you're just being saccharine sweet, but men don't pick up on this. If you're nasty, it'll show you feel threatened, and why would you? You're a much better catch than her and men are lining up round the street to take you out (as if! But it'd be nice, wouldn't it?). So show you're secure enough in yourself to be magnanimous. Ha!

Unfortunately, whilst issuing an invitation can be enough to make a woman back off, others are either too thick-skinned or determined to let the matter of a new girlfriend stand in their way. No matter. Look at it as if she is taking the bait.

As far as the Dish is concerned the message you will be transmitting to him is that you are a nice person. Sick. You are entertaining his former totty to a lovely meal. She will pick up *your* code. Something tells me that Charlie has been so busy concentrating on her career path that she would automatically think that people who cook are *hausfraus*. Her idea of entertaining is to treat a man to a meal at whatever spot the in-crowd are frequenting. She is indubitably going to turn out to be a trend follower and will not have developed her own sense of food style. Good! You should come out trumps then.

Canapés and cocktails are spot on because they will be quick and negate the painful experience of having the three of you sit together for too long at the table. By producing professional-standard canapés you will be demonstrating to both of them just how much you are in a different league to *Darling Charlie*. Stick to tonic yourself but let Snow White get as tanked up as she likes before dinner. My guess is she drinks an unladylike amount. No one has told her that you don't have to put away as much booze as a man.

Supper menu

Aperitif	Plymouth or Tanqueray Gin or Vodka with tonic and a selection of canapés.
Mini potato pancakes with smoked salmon and sour cream, vol au vent *cases with sour cream and mushrooms, red onion and goats cheese tarts*	You need to knuckle down and make these.
Thai chicken curry with rice	**Vampire rating 9**
Strawberry semi-fredo	Divine
Drink	The MOD's favourite beer.
Ambiance	Your song! The one when he first tried to kiss you at the party last summer.
Dress code	Cocktail dress and killer lashes – Charlie will be coming straight from work. This will highlight her crumpled, slightly sweaty appearance – you could suggest she 'freshens up' when she arrives if you like! It has been about a month since you have had a trim so get your barnet seen to.
Conversation	Believe me, what you don't say is going to be more important than what you do. Do not bring up work because she 'outguns' you on this. Nor who she is seeing in case this arouses the MOD's jealousy. Men sometimes feel proprietorial about an ex. If Charlie had anyone significant she would have brought him along. More likely she has come to give you the once over.

	How about not discussing your visitor at all? Talk about politics, religion, current affairs or what you and the Dish have been up to.

Canapés

The good news is that these are all really simple to make. The bad news is that it will take some time. Make the canapés ahead of time and freeze them. Then, it will only take 10 mins to finish off at 180 on the day.

Presentation must be first-rate. Put a generous amount of the pancakes on a serving plate and give each person a side plate and napkin, cocktail sized, if you can find them, otherwise normal.

Have extra ice for top-ups of drink in a bowl with a spoon. Slice lemon neatly for the drinks.

Vol au vent cases, tart shells

We could tell you how to make decent pastry cases but you know that this would be impossible (plum bottling must be avoided at all costs when there is a rival present). Buy some good quality ones.

Thai chicken curry

I found a great freebie handout from Sainsbury's a few years ago with a fantastic recipe for chicken curry. It was one of Jamie Oliver's. I can vouch for the fact that it will not dry up since the first evening I cooked it the husband rang me from a grass verge on the M1 coming back from Luton airport saying he had run out of petrol. I am used to this sort of thing. Tonight he's just working late. As I work away the darling is just leaving Croydon (it is 21: 56). Dinner is shrivelling in the oven by the minute. Like most men he seems unaware of the need to phone HQ when he is running behind.

PS This curry should be volcanically hot – you see Charlie will be somewhat flushed at the end of the evening. I do not think that is going to be very attractive!

Strawberry semi-freddo

I am really sorry about this, but on reflection, I cannot ask you to make this after all. I realise that both the MOD and the ex will be too pie eyed to appreciate your efforts. Keep your powder dry for another day and a more deserving guest.

If either of them is not legless, and expects pudding, slice a banana and squeeze over some lemon juice if you must.

P.S. Pre-book a cab. Aren't you organised?

Achievement and expectations

Be nice tomorrow. You can expect the MOD to have a hangover in the morning. I think Charlie will have understood you better after tonight.

SCORE

1. *Commitment*	5	He can't remember anything after 9 o'clock.
2. *Romance*	0	Brewer's droop.
3. *Fun*	11	Yes, yes, yes.

chapter 8

Reaching high command
How to win over the in-laws

As is the mother, so is her daughter.
Ezekiel XVi 4, Old Testament

Inspiration

Wholesome Anne in *Anne of Green Gables*. Go for a long walk around the block before the guests arrive to put some colour into your cheeks. No visible cleavage, minis, macros or high heeled peeptoe shoes with a marabou trim.

'Mum and dad are coming for lunch on Sunday to meet you' the MOD casually drops into the conversation. We do not have to spell out that a boyfriend's parents can put the kibosh on a budding romance. So, allow me to take complete charge. My dear girl, this is one encounter which has to be stage-managed in every respect.

When it comes to his parents there are few boundaries I would not cross to ingratiate myself. Before I snared my man my PML came up to a significant birthday and, to mark the occasion, I produced, virtually single handed, a supper for sixty of her closest friends. The effort nearly killed me but it was worth it. This was my grand gesture of devotion and it worked.

We will be expanding upon grand gestures in Chapter 15. Suffice to say here that men are suckers for largesse. Once you are in a relationship it would not occur to a man that you have any ulterior motive for being generous with your time or money— he will assume you are putting yourself out because you love him and recognise his worth. You do.

To be fair I have known a few chaps who tried hard to win my mother's vote. Their tactics included/led to the following:-

- Being bought *Ma Griffe* perfume.
  Yes, this worked.
- Receiving champagne for an anniversary.
  Yes.
- Accidentally having a car crash through the garage door into the back of dad's new Honda.
  No, Marcus.
- Attempting and botching DIY repair of sink.
  No, Marcus. Again. No.
- Ringing to ask after me when I did not want to know.
  Yes. Oh no.
- Being a doctor.
  David, Charles, Leo, Andrew. You bet.

Now that it is your turn to impress, keep it simple. Aim to act as if you were a rosy cheeked homebody.

Let's start at the beginning with the *mise en scène*. Mum will be forming her opinion of you in the first few seconds after she has stepped over the threshold. Everything she sees in those critical moments must be beyond reproach. You have already learned to keep the place spic and span. But, a Mother will *go out of her way* to find minor imperfections to reinforce her conviction that no one could conceivably look after, and by implication, care for her child (I know he's 32) as well as she could. She will scan your place for evidence, such as newsprinty fingerprints on white painted surfaces, to prove her point. Get on your knees and scrub that kitchen floor. All done?

Tip: Go outside and clean the outside of the front door.

Next, buy a nice bunch of petrol station blooms. A vase of £50 three foot tall amaryllis would be stunning but would make you look profligate.

This is not a red carpet occasion so you will not need the tablecloth either. Mats and neatly laid cutlery are all that is required. If you have a garden and can spare a couple of flowers why not pop them in a small jug in the centre? A sweet and feminine touch.

Unless mum and dad live around the corner – in which case the MOD would probably offer them some wine (empty the fridge of beer please), suggest a refreshing non-alcoholic pre-lunch drink to slake their thirst from the journey. On a really cold day, a nice cuppa would be a suitably dull drink to make. I would be minded to put the kettle on the moment I heard the doorbell then you can tell mum that the kettle's just boiling, would they care to join you in a cup of tea?

Now for the meal. What about the starter? There isn't going to be one. We will dispense with this since you really don't want to linger over this meal do you? I once served artichoke as an *hors d'oeuvre* to a friend's parents. This was a bum choice. The leaves are fiddly. You need a huge plate for them and it takes ages to finish. Unless you are getting on swimmingly you will exhaust small talk by the time the main course arrives. To cap it all, these parents, Brenda and Martin, were kosher and my ignorance of esoteric principles of kashrut was woefully exposed because I had made a sauce from melted butter. You are not supposed to do this if you are having meat as the main event. I scored a D.

the dish

Moving on to your main course, what do you think we will suggest? Arriving at the perfect choice involves a process of elimination. Avoid:

a) roasts because they are mum's territory,
b) lasagne/pasta because she might think this '*too studenty/ suggests that insufficient effort has been made over the meal*' – I agree – and
c) grilled fish because it can be smelly.

What's left? You have already done the shepherd's pie so switch to cottage pie in winter and infallible salmon poached in a *court bouillon* for a summer's day.

This main course will need to drown in vegetables to reassure Mother that her darling boy is getting his greens.

Just as you will be piling on the good stuff so you must rein in what the folks might consider to be pretentious or showy. This is not the occasion to demonstrate any interest in or knowledge of wine. Buy a supermarket (an upmarket one pls) own brand bottle – Claret (men of a certain age drink this) and a Chablis (because red wine probably gives mum a migraine, so have both available).

Should you drink? Absolutely. It is *imperative* that you do have one glass and one glass only. If you have none they will think you are in the family way. More than one, a slapper.

I asked my dear mother-in-law (a trained psychoanalyst) what she would like to see on this occasion. I thought that she would pick a dish she liked but no. She said that she would hope the girlfriend would make something she had learned from her own mother to enable her to form an idea of where this woman had come from. This is a fairly representative 'layered' response from my other 'mum'. Out of respect to Hermione I think you should do this. Shall we have a bit of fun? For the rest of this epic journey we are being careful to avoid you being seen as a PB. However, faced with the real thing, it seems obvious that the dish you attribute to your mother should be PLUM CRUMBLE!

You will at some stage have to let your mother into the subterfuge (or perhaps she really does make this) so that she does not drop you in it. And, lest you wonder why we do not make any provision in this book for meals with your parents, the rationale is that you are *not* going to cook for them. Your parents will be entertaining you.

Incidentally, in case you are curious about how I ingratiated myself with my better half's parents? I was lucky. I learned *en passant* that Lionel and Hermione had spent their first date at the White Tower in Charlotte Street in central London, a restaurant famed for its shallot and almond stuffed duck. It was pure fluke that the recipe for this unusual creation was in one of the sainted Robert Carrier books! I recreated their crunch-time meal. 10/10.

Now what do you make of this? Hermione's choice for an opening gambit when she entertained ME, was lobster eaten with special implements that look like the sort of thing my very handsome dentist, Russell, used on me when I had root canal treatment. I usually eat food with a knife and fork. On one level I suppose, this could be regarded as a delicacy. But, given the fact that it is difficult to extract the meat from the shell, I remain curious if this was a multi-faceted message as to my suitability. It brought to mind a review I read of a book about food and etiquette from the '40's, which I think was being republished, which mentions that cherries (or something like them – I can't really recall!!) were good to serve to an ex-spouse because of the conundrum posed by the stones.

Please do not think badly of me but I have what I maintain is a devilish streak although you may just think it puerile. I repaid mum-in-law in spades on her special birthday by inviting her to dip her feet into a washing up bowl filled with water when she crossed the threshhold. We said it was a symbolic gesture of rebirth.

Now, reverting to more serious matters, picture the following meals and imagine the conversation in the car when mum and dad are going home.

Mummy-pleasing Menu Dads have no independent view on food

No starter	On reflection, how about cut up Swedish herring on cocktail sticks?
Winter main course: Cottage pie with red cabbage, carrots, peas and cauliflower	**Vampire rating 1** The garlic content must be muted unless you know that they are used to eating garlic.
Summer main course: Whole salmon poached in a court bouillon *(poaching juice) with new potatoes, peas, carrots and cauliflower*	Respectable, but the fish will be sublimely moist because of the method of cooking it. Do not stint on the wine for the *court bouillon*. Bubble at least half a bottle of white with lemon juice, black pepper, a chopped onion and 2 chopped carrots for a minimum of 20 mins before immersing your fish. Add water and more wine as necessary and ladle the bouillon over the fish every so often to ensure the top is cooked too. Let the fish remain in the juice for as long as you can (best left overnight) before lifting it out.
Plum crumble	I find that adding grated lemon zest to the fruit gives the filling a zing. And you must sprinkle the topping with cinnamon because when you cook it the smell will fill the kitchen. Mummy will like this homely detail.
Drink	Supermarket Claret and Chablis. (For the salmon stick to the white.) Dad may like tonic water so buy some – not Schweppes but a no-frills slimline supermarket brand showing your thrift and giving a nod to your concern for the MOD's calorie intake.
Dress code	Something frumpy and floral from Laura Ashley that your mother bought you when you were a teenager. I had lots of things that

	would qualify. Go easy on the makeup and brush your hair. Avoid vampy nail varnish.
Ambiance	Music is last this time. Why? Brace yourself. It is going to be Wagner- anything in the Ring Cycle. Say you are saving up to go to Bayreuth (the music festival). Tickets are notoriously hard to come by so don't worry about having your bluff called.
Any other points	She will poke in the fridge so throw away anything mildewed or past its use by date. For once fill it to the gills with fruit and low fat cheese. And a cabbage. You know what roughage does for you don't you and mum will be thrilled to know you are mindful of sonny Jim's innards. The parents, like all their friends, will consume a Benecol (cholesterol reducing) product. You could do worse than buy one of these too.
Conversation	Let the MOD take the lead. It is better to appear to be on the timid and demure side. If you get mum alone in the kitchen you can tell her all about cooking!

Extra points to note

Vegetables
One word: immolated. Mums don't like *al dente* so boil greens to death. Dads don't like vegetables whichever way you do them so you may as well please one of them. Who do you think normally wears the trousers? Mum I think. Make her feel at home.

Carrots, peas and cauliflower
No minted carrots for the in-laws. We are striving for good honest,

unadulterated fare for this meal. They must be plain boiled like the peas and cauliflower please.

Summer salmon poached in a *court bouillon*

According to the Polish proverb *'Fish to taste right, must swim three times- in water, in butter and in wine'*. The secret to perfect, moist and delicately flavoured salmon lies in two ingredients – time and a fish kettle. It has got to be exemplary since Mum will be primed to gripe about your lack of cooking skills and how you dished out dried up fish.

One and a half hours to cook fish may sound like an age but, if you can make time to have your highlights touched up, you can surely make passable fish. As for the kettle, no need to panic if you do not own one. Buy or borrow it. A lot of supermarkets lend them free of charge. The fishmonger will give you the evil eye forever if you fail to return it spotless.

A good fishmonger or the person manning the fish counter is worth his weight in caviar. Only some serious grovelling kept me in with one of the charming and efficient team at a local supermarket fish counter two years ago. I pre-ordered three medium sized trimmed salmon for the Golden Wedding party which Stephen kindly offered to collect for me. He returned out of sorts with four mini whales and a sad tale of how the shop said that there was no one by the name of John whom I claimed to work there and certainly no order. Luckily, they had four fish out back. With fins.

When I unpacked the monsters all became clear because he had gone to the wrong shop by mistake. Communication not being our forte, I am sure that he was deeply engrossed in the FT when I gave him his instructions – his version was that I had just lost my marbles. We ended up with seven fish and served salmon to all visitors for the following month.

To ensure you hook your six foot fish make a good stock for Solly to swim in. The flavour will improve if you allow the fish to marinate in the bouillon for an hour after cooking or better still, overnight, before you skin it.

84

Vegetables

New potatoes can be seriously boring. Never mind. They will hit the right conservative note for the parents and at least you know that this version will be edible. You may wonder why I have not suggested my potato salad. The answer, of course, is that fathers prefer vegetables served hot. It would be odd to mix and match cold spuds with warm mixed veg. Furthermore, your oniony potato salad will give him wind.

Were you making the fish for a more youthful audience (it would go down well at big engagement party) we would suggest you made something refreshing and delicious like cous cous with broad beans and coriander.

Plum bottler's plum crumble*

Let yourself go mixing up the crumble topping for this pudding.

PS if his dad is anything like mine he will have a serious weakness for chocolate/choc ices. His wife probably does not let him have them at home because of the cholesterol content. Buy some and he will be rooting for you!

SCORE

1. *Commitment*	9	You are in the home straight.
2. *Romance*	6	He's a bit embarrassed.
3. *Fun*	1	They are the in-laws.

Plan B. Taste the plums when you get home and if they are floury, which plums can be, then I am afraid you will have to substitute apples for them in this recipe. You will have bought 3 good sized cooking apples just in case.

chapter 9

An army marches on its stomach
Breakfasts, brunches and light meals

"It takes some skill to spoil a breakfast – even the English can't do it"
John Kenneth Galbraith (1908-2006) American economist

Inspiration

Breakfast – Hilary Clinton. And she got and kept Bill.

Brunches – Madonna. Spirited, obviously a grafter. Probably knows you should be adorned with mascara from the moment you wake up. Always looks great.

Light Lunches – the girl who is your male colleagues' fantasy shag from the office – you can't go wrong by mimicking someone else's successful style. I bet she has a standing appointment to have her highlights done. The 'it girl' at work knows that with a bit of effort she can make herself indispensable in *and* outside work.

1. Breakfast

You will be getting up with the larks for this. Spring out of bed at dawn and head for the nearest farm. Collect freshly laid, still warm eggs. Sprint back home to finish off the masterpiece you have mapped out in your mind. Just as he is rousing you will be slinking back into the bedroom with a tray of scrambled eggs in one hand and a glass of chilled *Bollinger* in the other. Needless to say you will be wearing, as Marilyn Munroe said, nothing but Chanel No5!

I think that even he will be bored with this routine after several days.

You may think that breakfast is going to be an easy meal to get right. If so I doubt you have applied your mind to the *'real politique'*. We shall be working on two distinct messages here. Firstly, behind every successful man lies a woman. Your galvanising him for the day ahead is a clue that you will be a proactive asset to his career.

Second, even if you stack shelves at Tesco (nothing wrong with that mind you), you want to look motivated and you need the MOD to believe you have a demanding, fulfilling life outside of the relationship. A self-respecting career-minded woman never 'pulls a sickie' to spend mornings having leisurely breakfasts with her beau. Ergo, she has no intention of lingering over a coffee pot when she is expected elsewhere.

My advice is uncompromising. During the week PREPARE NO FOOD WHATSOEVER. Make your excuses and head off after your espresso. Let the Dish admire your work ethic.

The *one* thing you should do though is to make him his favourite beverage and give it to him when he wakes up so that he can enjoy it while shaving. Better put the cup on a tray if the carpet's white. Here, I do mean the favoured brand of tea, be it herbal, organic or even Fairtrade. Bless him! For coffee, the detail will impress if you either percolate, filter or cafetière the preferred brew. Unless he insists, do not bother with decaff. Nasty stuff. For me it is just discoloured water.

Tip: If you are staying over at his place make sure *you* leave first if you do not have keys. Before I got to the stage of being given a spare set Stephen forgot I was in the house and locked me in. I was trapped; the window in the front overlooked a drop down to basement level so there was no way I could climb out. My predicament would not have been too grim but for the fact that he was headed to Frankfurt. It was embarrassing to ring his PA, Lisa, and ask her if she could send someone across town to release me. Plus, I had some awkward explaining to do at the office when I pitched up three hours late.

The weekend is the time to be flexible. As a sound *modus operandi*, scout around for a good deli for freshly-made croissants, crisp rolls or *proper* bagels. As distinct from rolls with holes. They should be crisp on the outside and chewy inside. My experience is that all of these bread stuffs are programmed to turn mysteriously soggy between 2-3 am so there is no point buying them in advance.

Every so often go the whole nine yards and make the lad a full English breakfast. If he is headed off to football, hockey or golf it will make you look considerate if you whip up a fortifying morning meal before he leaves. And it will be less likely that he will linger in the clubhouse after his game for a BLT and a quick flirt with some totty. You don't need this. If it is anything like my tennis club it could be prime 'pick up' territory for singletons. He could be exposed to legions of unattached, macro skirted, skorted and generally leggy, attractive, professional accountants, doctors, solicitors, barristers etc, etc. Do I need go on?

While it is essential to execute a cooked breakfast well you are not running a hotel. There is no need to provide a choice of eight dishes on hot plates served under silver domes – unless (1) this is a posh weekend house party (2) you happen to live in a stately home and (3) have live-in uniformed staff. I have never been to one of these events (= I *am* angling for an invite here but do you mind if I bring along the children – and a small dog or two, the cat and my daughter's favourite doll – whoops – and the husband).

I do not blame my other half if he is occasionally troubled that I unaccountably forget he exists. I confess that when I was doing the table plan for the top table at our wedding I was one man short. I had omitted the groom. This was not tit for tat for the German trip.

To ensure an enjoyable experience takes a modicum of effort on your part. I would suggest that you made a visual impact with a 'spread'. Men like a sea of bottles on the table- tomato ketchup, brown sauce and mustard, not forgetting marmite, two kinds of jam and marmalade to accompany toast.

Remember nice touches such as having butter in a butter dish, toast in a basket or rack. This is the perfect moment to dust off the teapot. An embroidered tea cosy would be kitsch not 'ironic'.

Those were the Do's. There is only one don't. Avoid noxious fish such as kippers as you will reek like a trawler all day.

Finally, if you make a traditional breakfast, skip a full lunch. The Dish will not appreciate it. We have prepared a list of superb light meals to make instead.

Cooked breakfast options

Full English	Eggs, bacon, sausage, tomato – I don't bother with mushrooms or beans. Baked beans at this hour of the day conjure up a *tableau* of a sad English breakfast which I was astounded to see being served in a colonial style hotel in Spain patronised almost exclusively by British SAGA age clients.

	I know it is nice to have all the comforts of home when you travel, but, in a hot climate I would have thought that a continental style meal would have been more appropriate. I suppose I should not have been too surprised though. The previous evening part of the live entertainment featured an enthusiastic rendition of the 'hokey cokey'!
Scrambled eggs with smoked salmon or mushrooms	Use a *bain marie* for making the scrambled eggs – and add a dash of cream. Unless you know they are first rate, avoid supermarket mushrooms which can lack the texture and earthy flavour of market or greengrocer produce.
Drink	Are you serious?
Ambiance	Just the rustle of the *Sunday Times*.
Dress code	Imagine the front door bell is ringing first thing in the morning and you open up to find the assembled flashlights of the paparazzi. Now what image of yourself would you like to see on the front pages of the nationals? Use your discretion but absolutely no towelling robes or pyjamas. It is time for the silk negligee that has been sitting in your cupboard for five years. And, on your tootsies there should be no bed socksies or 'novelty' slippers adorned with reindeer or similar designs. Find something grown up or, failing this, go barefoot. I can understand a friend of ours looking under whelmed when given a coral coloured towelling robe for Christmas by her

	boyfriend, soon to be fiancé. If this is what she was to be adorned with at the zenith of his passion, what alluring gifts can he be giving her now? Something householdy I expect.
Conversation	Best not to expect too much lively discussion first thing in the morning. I have already disclosed the fiasco with the fish. Has this sort of thing happened to you too? Perhaps the penny has not dropped yet that men do not multi-task. If they are reading a paper or a book you will be lucky to get a grunt in response to a question. This is not personal. Sarah agrees. She says that she could announce that she's running off with the milkman when Peter is reading his paper and there would be no response at all. Except his 15 second auditory memory kicks in after a bit and he says, 'Hmm?' My husband claims to have read somewhere that it is to do with the way a male brain is wired. When one lobe is occupied with a 'doing' task the receiving part of the cerebellum is programmed to filter out particular impulses, coincidentally, ones which are at the same pitch as a nagging woman's voice. This sounds like what my grandmother would have called a 'bubbe meiser' (= a cross between a fib and nonsense).
Any other points?	Nagging. Following on from the above, men are also pathologically allergic to what they perceive to be nagging. Do not say to the

	MOD at breakfast something like 'You haven't taken out the rubbish yet', 'Would you mind not putting your dirty clothes back in the cupboard' or 'can't you remember to take your muddy shoes off before you step on the kitchen floor'. The last one really gets Stephen's goat particularly if I repeat it two minutes later. I have a genetic predisposition to doing this. My definition of nagging is that it is the repetition of unpalatable truths. Collins say it is 'to worry by constant fault-finding'. Oh dear.

Full English

Comment

A bit of legwork beforehand transforms fried food from greasy spoon into superior fare.

Bangers

Rubbery flavourless sausages are a turn off. Buy only the best premium ones. By far the most succulent variety I have polished off came from local Suffolk-reared pigs near Nicole's 'weekend' place. She owns a rather austere stone building in the middle of nowhere not a million miles from a nuclear power station. This is prime pig farming territory. Maybe nuclear reactors and juicy sausages go hand in hand. Anyway, I loved her bacon and plump sausages but am not convinced they outweighed the disadvantage of living near swine. Flies. She should have bought somewhere next to arable farming land.

Back to the range. How you cook sausages will make all the difference. I am certain that the texture of the meat is better if they are pan fried rather than oven baked or grilled. Prick them or they will explode! All the same I tend to use a lid to minimize collateral spattering.

Avoid getting egg on your face
Like the curate's legendary *oeuf* they can be good in parts. I find that fried ones turn to fibreglass with whites horribly welded to the pan and the yolk incinerated around the edges. Tried poaching? This is a more interesting and frankly, reliable, technique. I suppose you could just toss an egg into swirling water and hope for the best but I fear the resulting goo will resemble the outcome of a failed experiment from an adolescent's chemistry set. What you really need is an inexpensive poaching ring to prevent it disintegrating.

The only other option is to scramble. You really ought to try doing this in the *bain marie*.

Plum bottling alert! A sprig of parsley adorning a mound of creamy scrambled eggs could be your undoing because it might appear as if (a) you are trying *too* hard and (b) you had this meal all planned to down to the last 'T'. The idea for brekkie is to show that you can rustle up something delicious *spontaneously*.

PS forget about boiled eggs. They are dull. Keep them for the sick room.

A word about toast
The finest bread for making toast is undoubtedly brown. This is perfect not because it is healthy – this is irrelevant- but because it is more likely to taste of something. Toast should be made at the last minute when the rest of breakfast is ready because it gets cold so quickly.

Put aside your dislike of this loathsome spread and buy a jar of marmite. For some reason men love it.

2. Brunch

Brunch, being eaten mid to late morning, can be a more substantial event than breakfast. It also means you can dispense with lunch. Most significantly from the male perspective, the sun is closer to going down over the yard arm, so it is acceptable to serve alcohol. Whoopee!

This is one of those 'coupley' meals – you know what I mean- cafes are chokka with starving tousled twosomes with 'bed hair'. The trouble I have found is that, by the time you *have* got out of bed, anywhere good is heaving and you have to queue for a table which ends up being too miniscule to unfold the paper. So, Miss, you are going to have a stab at making a decent mid-morning brunch in the comfort of your home.

Drink
He may be in desperate need of a 'hair of the dog'.

What do you serve? Not what you think. I reckon that you are half way to the cupboard to fetch a bottle of bubbly. Stop! Remember, champagne or Bucks Fizz are discounted for the reason already given in Chapter 2.

A superior choice would be a bloody Mary made, of course, with genuine Russian vodka and a cocktail shaker. I understand that the key to this drink lies in a liberal dose of freshly squeezed lemon juice and ice. Mix in some Tabasco and Worcester sauce to taste. And remember to avoid juices made from concentrate.

Orange juice
Some men over 30 suddenly mutate into health freaks. If so they will do one or more of the following:-

- get up at 5.30 to work out every day before going to the office
- be more consistent about avoiding butter with bread

95

and puddings at a restaurant than you
• start to read biographies of famous dictators and
• often lose their sense of humour.

Perhaps it suddenly dawns on them that one day we all have to die. Anyway, I know a perfectly nice chap who might qualify for this syndrome. He is not what *I* would call a laugh a minute. Actually he has regaled me at least once with the story about his structural problems and his campaign to truncate licensing hours at his local watering hole.* I am more interested in finding out what has driven his neighbours to the pub. If this sort of unfortunate transformation has taken place in your MOD I am sorry but skip to the next section and pour him a long drink of orange juice.

Assuming your boyfriend has not discovered the facts of life (and death) do not ruin his breakfast by pouring him a glass of OJ or some weird concoction like kiwi blended with celery, carrot and wild dandelion seeds which you have heard from your best friend is great for kick starting a detox regime. Hideous. He will not want to have you thrust healthy drinks at him on a Sunday morning when he is enjoying himself.

Food

What would you think is fitting for a late morning meal? We are still on that learning curve aren't we? Avoid the obvious – replicating the breakfast menu, and choose something more esoteric. Vanessa, a shrewd friend says she consciously opted for sherried mushrooms on toast to wow her new boyfriend, now (loaded) husband and his friends at brunch. They now need to arrange their diaries carefully so they can spend 'quality time' at (a) a fab house in central London (b) a fab country cottage for *le weekend* and (c) a fab house within easy commuting distance of Bloomingdales. New York, dear. Well done! Incidentally, she also updated his work clothes and (what a relief this must have been) did away with his centre parting. The well known saying 'behind every successful man lies a woman' surely

---

*I really must make more of an effort to inject some enthusiasm into normal, earnest conversations of this nature. See more on this in Chapter 12.

applies to this couple. Personally, I like Stephen's version of this home truth – 'behind every unsuccessful man lies an angry woman'.

Apologies. I digress. Unless you live in Cornwall, where freshly caught mackerel is sweet and juicy, pause before serving this fish because it is usually horrid. I know one accomplished cook who suffered from some kind of mental aberration in her menu choice for her celebration weekend nosh. *Al fresco* dinner on Saturday night featured what I regarded as nasty mackerel with potato salad and lentils. The rainy *al fresco* Sunday brunch was MORE nasty mackerel with potato salad and lentils. A number of adults (you guessed – us) were seen raiding the kiddies tepee for their sandwiches and sweets. Variety is essential when entertaining guests for more than one meal.

Mea culpa.

Do better with any of the following:

Eggs benedict	Poached eggs + ham + hollandaise on muffin.
Spanish omelette	**Vampire rating 1**
Scotch pancakes with scrambled eggs	
Drink	Bloody Mary- make sure you have put the ice tray in the freezer the night before.
Ambiance	Chopin or other piano concertos.
Dress code	Designer sweat pants and co-ordinated top from Sweaty Betty/ go nautical with a stripy top and white, well cut jeans. NO TRAINERS. They whiff after a while, are ugly and make most people look stunted. Pretty sandals with a heel will give a better line. Alternatively, flip flops and nothing in winter – you are indoors after all.

Any other points?	Yes- send him out to buy some fresh croissants and the paper when he is dressed. Then, he can return to the smell of sizzling butter as he opens the front door.
For dessert, a palate cleanser in the form of a bowl of mixed red berries is a refreshing way to end the meal.	Nice and light. Or, in a short window in the summer where apricots are tangy, serve these with strong black coffee and Turkish delight. In what I claim to be down to false memory syndrome, I thought that the partnering of apricots and coffee was inspired by one of Sean Connery's outings as 007. Stephen – a walking Bond nerd – can pinpoint the morning meal I mean to the 51st minute of *From Russia With Love* ('of course') and it was fresh figs with yoghurt. This sounds quite nice too.
Conversation	Take the initiative dear.

Good stuff. The Dish, if he has any sense, will warm to all of these options. They show you to be able to make something which is not run of the mill. Being able to scatter the sections of the paper around the room will be a bonus.

Do we have a view as to which of these dishes you should plump for first? My husband's preference would be the American style brunch dish of eggs Benedict (it makes him wistful for his single days in Manhattan), but the other two are equally tasty. The former is essentially a poached egg served on a thick wedge of ham or bacon and a muffin and then smothered in Hollandaise sauce.

A Spanish omelette is an omelette enlivened by incorporating a mix of vegetables and/or cooked meat. A tasty way of using up leftovers. For a long time I did not know what this dish was. I once asked someone and they said it was like something else. Since I had not got a clue what this was either I was none the wiser. I now use the term, a '*Spanish omelette*' to denote an explanation which makes no sense. I used to think that a former boss at work excelled at this but it was probably me being obtuse.

My third brunch recommendation is Scotch pancakes with scrambled eggs. You will like this since I will wager you have a sweet tooth. Aside from the flavour, the plus point here is that you can make the pancake mixture the night before and leave it in a jug in the fridge. The pancakes will only take a couple of minutes to fry in butter.

I made this when my husband's veggie friend came to stay after a stint in the West Bank working for some sort of tree hugging peace movement she supports. She is delightfully eccentric. She is big on women's rights and world peace. I like her immensely, but I am beginning to find myself harbouring ungenerous thoughts because she once turned up close to midnight having mislaid our address. Last time she arrived having hitched a lift from a complete stranger in an old army truck. I hope her timekeeping is better when she has to broker a ceasefire somewhere.

She has just hosted a vegetarian birthday party at a retreat in Devon. The centrepiece of the menu was a curried lentil log. I bring this up for the benefit of any vegetarians, vegans or pescetarians. I feel strongly that, even if you hold to a particular diet, it is wrong to inflict your choice on guests who may not enjoy it. Unless it is wonderful, with or without meat, as some veggie dishes are (anything with Feta, for example). Next time I will take ham sarnies.

SCORE

1. *Commitment*	7	An easy one to get right.
2. *Romance*	7	He's better in the morning.
3. *Fun*	7	Not a bad way to pass time.

3. Light meals, snacks and cold collations

Your goal here is to titillate his taste buds when he feels like never eating again. Like Pavlov's dog the MOD will begin to salivate when you approach the kitchen and be wondering what delicious new treat you have in store for him next.

The medley of dishes we have collated are perfect for lunchtime if you are feeling bloated after a big blow out at breakfast. They would equally suit an early evening or late night snack.

1. Proper Welsh Rarebit.	
Drink	Serve with chilled red Sancerre or other Loire red.
2. Sliced cold fillet of beef with celeriac remoulade and crusty bread	**Vampire rating 4**
Drink	As above.
3. Smoked salmon with marinated fennel and asparagus	
Drink	Gros Plante de Nantes or other Muscadet.
4. Bought chicken liver pâté with sliced mountain salami, beef tomato, fresh bread	Serve with 'Aunt Jessica's' onion marmalade.
Drink	Serve with chilled Rose d'Anjou.
5 Pasta with a chilli, lemon and garlic sauce	**Vampire rating 4** Fry 2 chopped red chillies with 4 chopped garlic cloves in oil. Pour over the pasta

	having first doused it in a cup of cooking liquid and the juice of one English bought lemon or half a Mediterranean one brought back from your holiday. I often fill my suitcase with luscious lemons.
6. Greek salad	Only if it is baking outside. We would both use Cos rather than round lettuce unless this comes from a farm or stall. Really fresh lettuce has a trace of flavour and texture, qualities which can be horribly absent from some greenery.
7. Prawn cocktail	Didn't this used to be the nation's favourite starter followed by curry?
Drink	To show you have a sense of humour about wine, serve this with that '70's classic, Mateus Rose.
8. Avocado and Parma ham with freshly shaved parmesan	Drizzle over some balsamic.
Drink	Gros Plante de Nantes or other Muscadet.
9. Pasta with pesto sauce	**Vampire rating 5**

1.   Proper Welsh Rarebit

The Dish will appreciate this on a bitterly cold Sunday night. It has a magical quality – men find it is hard to resist. Practical too, since you can prepare the topping ahead of time.

A delightful surprise is that the red wine can be served cold. I doubt he has ever tried this before. However, I can attest that, unlike Beaujolais Nouveau, which is to my mind a gimmick, this refreshing and vibrant wine really works.

2. Sliced cold fillet of beef with celeriac remoulade and crusty bread

I came across this 'combo' at a delightful old fashioned hotel in Arras, *l'Hotel de l'Universe*, where it was served as part of wedding celebrations. After twenty four hours of solid feasting the British contingent was close to defeat. But, the buffet, comprised of slabs of garlicky pink flesh, accompanied by remoulade and chilled red wine revived the jaded palate. We tucked in.

I really impressed my husband that weekend by having the foresight to bolt out of the reception to bag another bedroom having learned that the courtyard we overlooked was going to reverberate with a disco from a second function. It pays to do your homework if you are staying somewhere with several dining suites. Then you will get a good night's sleep and the MOD will be amazed by the fact that you are so street savvy.

This is going to be a five star supper dish. The beef is made in the same way as for the 'base-camp' meal. The key to succulent cold meat is two-fold. First, pack it with garlic cloves. Second, carve it at the last minute. This is why you must not buy sliced cooked meat.

The joint needs to be roasted for a minimum period only. Spike with loads of garlic and slather with oil before roasting. Make sure you have English mustard on hand.

To achieve a perfect texture with celeriac shred it in a machine. A grater generates unappetising, watery mulch. Scout's honour, I have also tried to slice it by hand but I get bored half way through and am left with rather unpleasant chunks that no one in their right mind would find tempting.

3. Smoked salmon with marinated fennel and asparagus

This is seriously classy and you will recall, if you were paying attention, that this amazing item was amongst the lunch choices for the WAGS in Chapter 4. Today smoked salmon is no longer a delicacy. As a corollary, it must be first rate (i.e. expensive/organic/ wild) or served innovatively. While you can get away with regular packet salmon it is never worth using anaemic thin spears of asparagus.

Supermarkets can be great. But, for real intensity of flavour and texture– for essentials such as herbs, fruit and vegetables, cheese and even cooked meat, cast your shopping net wider. Explore a proper market, farm shops and local greengrocers.

Living in a city we have concluded that the best places for buying tasty and inexpensive fruit and vegetables are stalls outside stations or markets. I do not mean 'Farmers Markets' which I find ersatz and expensive and the atmosphere somewhat 'earnest'. Too middle class and green wellied. It does not frankly bother me if the wares are locally sourced or come from Timbuktu. Sarah is a bit more 'food miles' aware!

Befriend a couple of stallholders, engage in a bit of repartee (it helps if you know which football team they support) – learn their names. I trust one particular fruit and veg expert (a real barrow boy) from Islington's Chapel Street Market to tell me what is tastiest, ripest and best. Whenever I cater for a large party I place an order for my fruit and vegetable requirements with him knowing that it will all be ready – in tip top condition – for collection. He is the best! The bottom line is that I am getting the same personal attention as I would at the finest shop – perhaps better.

I also cannot praise too highly the *fromage* men who sell cheese with guts. The only downside is that if I am with Stephen, intent on purchasing one solitary item, inevitably we egg each other on to buy a vat full of ripe, smelly cheeses. Like many fit men, Stephen monitors his cholesterol intake and normally eschews hard cheese. Poor thing, I often tease him when he is in diet mode by wafting a slice of glistening gorgonzola on toast under his nose to test his resolve. He is powerless to resist.

I digress. This is how I would serve smoked salmon to passengers on the Orient-Express' sister train, the British Pullman. I have only been once and this was for a day out to the Goodwood Revival. It was fantastic. Our generous host, Paul, hired an entire carriage as an unusual venue for his, hmm, (50th) birthday celebrations. Everyone had to wear 1940's or 1950's dress and they started serving shampoo with breakfast.

The décor was amazing even in the (immaculately clean) loo. My only two complaints were first, the smoked salmon served with breakfast was generous and of good quality but, in my opinion, served in a somewhat pedestrian manner. Safe and inoffensive I suppose. I can't help thinking that the sumptuous surroundings deserved something more elaborate. Oh – and you guessed it - the coffee was, in my (caffeine addict's) opinion, weak.

4. Chicken liver pâté with sliced mountain salami, beef tomato, fresh bread and 'Aunt Jessica's' onion marmalade

Pâté
I know an amazing method for making chicken liver pâté. I would like to pretend it originated from a restaurant in the Haute Savoie on a skiing trip a few years back but this would be a whopper. It was on the back of a packet of frozen chicken livers from Sainsbury's. I suppose it is academic because I would not share my secret with you – Plum Bottler, Plum Bottler, Plum Bottler! *You do not* make pâté, you buy it.

Men like spicy pickled things, so ask Aunt Jessica if she can spare some of her onion marmalade or pickled fruit for you. I keep some of the former bottled (Ahem, a PB!) in a sterilised jar in the fridge.

*A brief word about slicing onions. My eyes water terribly when I peel and slice onions. If this happens to you too then, can I suggest you either perform this operation out of doors (which I try and do even in mid-winter) or you apply mascara after the chopping/slicing part of the recipe is completed.

**A slightly less brief word about grenadine syrup, an essential ingredient of onion marmalade. Is it me, or are there two entirely different products which could both be grenadine syrup? Which one is intended for this recipe I do not know but I am partial to only one of them. The first product is pale brown in colour and looks very liquidy. I can't help thinking that this belongs in your rum punch. The second, which I always put in the 'confit', is called molasses de grenadine. I would suspect that this translates as grenadine syrup too wouldn't you? But this one is dark and viscous.

***To pickle fruit you need copious amounts of white wine vinegar. Two summers ago my parents dumped on me kilos of apples from their tree to convert into chutney. I sent Stephen out to buy 10 bags of sugar and 10 bottles of vinegar and he returned a bit pale. Given the levels of heightened security we live under he was worried that, much as men might get a second look if they purchased 50 tubs of peroxide from the hairdresser's, so he felt that he had been regarded suspiciously at the check-out for loading up his trolley with this lot. Come to think of it the telephone sounds a bit 'hollow' from time to time. MI5 must now know my secrets - (a) the perfect recipe for chutney *and* (b) who is the dishiest doctor in town.

6. Greek salad
We are really not sure about this one. It may go down well on a hot day but it is a bit girly. I suppose it reminds me of a week I spent with another girl friend, Elizabeth, in Eilat. We splurged on the accommodation, and I was dying for fish, but Greek salad was the only item on the menu of the fancy hotel that I could afford. After 14 servings you can understand that, by the end of the holiday, I felt like doing a dance like Anthony Quinn in *Zorba the Greek*.

On the other hand, as Sarah points out, it has raw red onions in i.e. hot hot hot! And men like that. Also, she says, it may be a sperm thing (sorry!) but men seem to like salty foods e.g. feta, capers, salted nuts, anchovies, things 'in a salt crust' (and tangy things like gherkins, while we're at it), so she thinks it'll go down well.

The only way I would make this now would be if I had a jar of 'full-blooded' feta cheese in the fridge. To make this, marinate ordinary packet feta cheese with oil and fresh thyme (ideally for several days) to lend a more piquant flavour. WARNING! This is done in a glass jar. Ergo plum bottling. Do not let on.

7. Prawn cocktail

We are confident that the MOD will not have eaten an entirely home made and assembled prawn cocktail before. This will not change with you either since we are not proposing that you cook, then shell prawns. But he will love eating this classic.

Buy any cooked prawns (so long as they are well within their sell-by date) from a reputable supermarket. 'Marie Rose' sauce is a doddle to whip up and absolutely delicious. The *really* quick method is ketchup and salad cream! But look online or dig in a good cookery book for a fancier recipe.

8. Avocado and Parma ham with freshly shaved parmesan

Can you handle this one solo?

9. Pasta with pesto sauce

No point buying this sauce. Basil loses its unique punch if it is stored in a jar. This is a CookSmart special – you can't mess it up if you have fresh basil and garlic, parmesan, pine nuts and oil. Just tip in the amounts you want until it tastes right to you. To make the sauce you need preferably a mortar and pestle, alternatively improvise and use a bowl and the end of a rolling pin. If you don't have one or find this too taxing, give up and shove everything in the blender. Sarah's telling me to remind you to leave the basil stalks out though.

NB. A short word about sauces and vinaigrettes

Can you explain to us why you have got a bottle of Thousand Island dressing in the cupboard? Salad cream and ketchup are the only ready made sauces you should have. Oh well, and Dijon mustard I suppose.

But we will not hear any lame excuse as to why you have not made the vinaigrette. You do not need to have done a Rick Stein cookery master class to knock this sort of thing up in seconds.

Vinaigrettes are by and large incredibly easy to make provided that you have olive oil, white wine vinegar, mustard powder, lemon juice and honey. You will naturally have all of these ingredients on hand.

PS Crispbreads

For less elaborate snacking, make sure that you have a box of oatcakes, flat breads or plain digestives in the cupboard. This is the perfect base for a variety of toppings. According to my husband, men do not touch ryvita or other crisp breads. Unless, like Sarah's husband, they are Swedish, in which case it's compulsory. Likewise cottage cheese – except when the in-laws are coming to town.

SCORE

1. Commitment	7	Not a pizza in sight. He liked these.
2. Romance	6	Infrequent but good.
3. Fun	6	Alright.

chapter 10

In the field –
Al fresco dining
Picnics and barbecues

"The wasp to your lips still follows with fretful persistence"
The Englishman in Italy
Robert Browning (1812-1889) English poet and playwright

Inspiration

Grace Kelly. Again! This is going to be hard to swallow but not that many people look great in jeans. You need a tight behind. I wonder if Ms Kelly wore them at all? I am not inferring that she did not have a fabulous *derriere,* just that living in France she would have been exposed to the stylish examples of ordinary women looking chic in their casual wear. French gals are often seen down the market (the Casino supermarket as well as *le marché)* sporting well-cut nautical-inspired navy trews or cream slacks and nice tops – not just ugly, androgynous vesty things, strappy tops revealing a grey bra and shapeless cover-ups.*

Picnics are alluring *in principle*. They conjure up a romantic notion of eating in a convertible car under a piercing blue sky, a soft pine scented breeze and chicken legs wrapped in napkins being produced from an old fashioned cold box. Grace Kelly and dreamy Carey Grant in *'To Catch a Thief'*.

Picture this if you will.

Your heart soars. He has called at work to say that he is going to whisk you off to the *Côte d'Azure* for the weekend! Then he informs you that he is seeing a client in Watford on Friday afternoon so can you get up to Luton under your own steam where you will be flying Easyjet to Nice?

We know what you are thinking. Cheapskate. But, discount airlines are not the end of the world, precious one. Easyjet planes are clean and flight crews friendly. As for Luton, if you told your colleagues that this is where you were going they might be impressed. Yes. Over dinner with a delightful and sophisticated chap, Lucian and his as always elegant wife, Madison (we were assured that her real life wacky name was real – at first we thought she had changed it from Karen) two years ago I learned that private jets departed from Luton. In fact they announced with a certain swagger, that the following Wednesday this is precisely how *they* were to travel to Geneva at a cost I believe of some £9,000.

Do you see a pattern beginning to emerge with the giving of additional information to impress (remember the villa that 'sleeps 10')? Just mentioning a private flight was clearly not enough. All I can say is that the experience must have been a be truly amazing one to warrant a long trek to Luton since the couple in question lived minutes from Heathrow Airport.

---

*If you need upholstering, buy a strapless bra please. Or those fabulous vests with an integral underwired bra – Sarah LOVES these. Incidentally, if you are a C cup or larger, *always* wear a bra.

Surprise the Dish with your reaction to his invitation. Who wants an uninspiring in-flight meal anyway? Well, I say meal. It'll be an acceptable snack that you have to pay for. Instead, make a delectable picnic. As my family and I jetted off on an orange plane not so long ago we drew envious glances from fellow passengers as we wolfed down our feast – cold flavoursome sausages, ham sandwiches on fresh granary bread, juicy sweet apricots and designer crisps. In our time we have also put away fantastic cold lamb sandwiches with mustard on the train in the Channel tunnel. Sublime.

1. The picnic

In the main picnics will be spur of the moment because they are weather dependent. It is tempting to think that, simply because the sun shines, everything will take care of itself. Hellooo. Since when has optimism been part of a CookSmart's regime? A smart cook knows that, if anything, having your meal outside requires *more* thorough planning than eating in familiar surroundings. Ask the MOD – he's an Arsenal fan and can tell you that away games are particularly difficult to win.

In order to be remotely enjoyable, devote an evening to going through your mental checklist of the chief components of a perfect 'spontaneous' *al fresco* meal – equipment, food and venue.

Reverting to sport a minute – make sure your plans do not clash with a crucial match. He won't be joining you on your outdoor feast if there is a major league tournament on offer. Nor in the mood for romantic outings if England are trying to qualify. Can I suggest that you get hold of a fixtures list?

Equipment

Your picnic will be stylish. Think along the lines of the decadent Russian luncheon scene in Maxim Gorky's *'Summer Folk'* – dappled sunlight, blankets spread out *à l'herbe*, wickerwork, bottles of chilled *champagnska* (Russian Champagne – it doesn't travel, so don't bother seeking it out, says Sarah, who brought some back from a gap year only to find it was like turps after six months) and wild strawberries. This translates as no leftover lurid coloured paper plates or cheap plastic cups emblazoned with balloons and screaming 'Party!' at you. Nor service station plastic utensils.

Baskets

What do you intend to use to transport food, plates, cutlery and glasses? A carrier. Wrong answer. The only reason you will have two plastic bags is that one is for rubbish and the other to store soiled plates and cutlery.

Baskets are robust and look good. Mums always have several. Your beloved will also feel manly being asked to carry it, striding over the meadows etc. Filch one now. Unless the MOD has had a hernia, let him display his chivalrous side and hump it about.

Crockery, cutlery and glassware

I thoroughly enjoyed a seriously posh picnic on a friend's motor boat near Henley. The hostess, Louise, is an amazing cook and even the intermittent rain did not dent our enjoyment of her fabulous lunch. I vaguely recall a gamey stew and summer pudding? It says something about me that I would be able to give you chapter and verse about the meal had it been poor. But what has remained ingrained in my memory of the occasion was the fact that she had gone to the trouble of using chinaware. It made us feel quite special. Now, this would be nice for you too but *de trop* in the dating context.

At Henley Regatta Sarah said that she heard the car park ringing with people unpacking tureens, tables and chairs and vases of flowers (she kids you not) and asking each other 'More sprouts darling?' So you can go too far in transporting your whole dining room to the country. The only china I would bother with are cups for coffee since this is disgusting drunk from plastic.

It is not hard to find stylish plastic plates. By all means transport food in Tupperware but, for an elegant effect, eat off something that does not bend when you put food on it. I would give you a red card now if you showed up with paper plates. So will the MOD, who will not take well to having an oily stain on the pale blue 'Andrew Pant' he bought from Bloomingdales.

Proper cutlery is essential. Either use an everyday set or buy some cheap and cheerful ones.

Finally, glasses. There is no need to take grandma's crystal. They would be a nightmare to cart across fields *and* are fragile. For the boating outing Louise's mooring was conveniently sited next to the car park so we could easily negotiate the short journey from boat to boot with all the paraphernalia for an upmarket luncheon party. For you, plastic flutes will do.

Belt and braces

Staying with drink, lukewarm beverages are foul. Take every precaution to keep drink cool since you are unlikely to find somewhere to buy cold drinks out in the sticks. Wrap bottles in those iced freezer contraptions *and* buy an insulated lunch box.

À table or à terre?

The really big decision. In my single days I was invited to Glyndebourne several times. The first occasion was with Dan (a successful solicitor - my mother *really* liked him), whose friend owned a convertible vintage car. I haven't a clue what make but it was black and came with a good sized, nifty built-in table making dining a grand experience high above the *'hoi palloi'*.

Another time Tim (yet *another* lawyer *noch* (=indeed)), who you know is toxically opposed to most vegetation *schlepped* (= dragged around) a folding table, tablecloth and chairs miles to the picnic area. Like a pillock I stupidly lugged a candelabra behind him forgetting it is too light for candles in broad summer and when the opera is finally over you can't wait to jump in the car and head back to civilization.

I can therefore tell you that hauling furniture and furnishings around the country is *pointless*. The essence of a picnic is a degree of informality it is virtually impossible to create indoors. Unless you have an Old Roller, stretch out on a tartan rug and have eats within reach. Do you have a travelling rug? If not, try mum again and if she has one with a waterproof reverse, all the better. By the way, avoid ethnic style dyed rugs. I once ruined a pair of pink trousers sitting on a friend's hand dyed orange rug at an outdoor concert. The grass must have been slightly damp and the colour ran. That was the writing on the wall for another potential squeeze, Adam.

NB you will be kicking yourself if you forget to pack corkscrew, napkins and kitchen roll to mop up the inevitable spills. If you are in the garden, attractive food umbrellas/covers (and a fly swot) are always useful.

Venues

Unless either of you has a particular location in mind the MOD's halcyon vision of the perfect outdoor lunch could be ruined. For a girl in *your* situation you cannot afford to leave matters to random chance. He will have been on countless run-of-the mill picnics. Surprise him by suggesting somewhere. How will he know you have carried out a recce when he was away on business?

If you have no better ideas, why not on impulse (huh!) suggest somewhere close to home, avoiding a long car journey? How about the back garden, a local park, or, hmm, the bedroom.

Not that we are Bible bashers, but the Good Book occasionally contains practical advice (you have to extrapolate its meaning out of context in this instance - and we mean no offence, since we know the author was not thinking of something as trivial as picnic arrangements) but it does say that *'stolen waters are sweet, and bread eaten in secret is pleasant'*. Could this not be interpreted as an endorsement of indoor picnics – there is something furtive about the notion, isn't there? And fun.

Arguably the best picnics I have had recently have taken place inside my lurid orange two-man Milletts tent, now pitched permanently in the back garden during summer months. For reasons hard to fathom, it entices visitors, irrespective of age, to leap inside and zip up the 'front door'.

I confess that late in the evening it is quite fun also to slip into the tent with coffee and a bottle of wine and listen to the birds tweeting away.

Picnic food

To pin down Mr ACII (it's the accountancy qualification, stoopid!) you must shun coleslaw, marinated artichokes or red peppers in little plastic pots which leak greasy oil, boring pasta, dull salads and tedious salmon. What's left?

Never fear. Aunt Jess and the pair of us will together get you out of the culinary hole. We have come up with a list of *first class picnic fare* – it will both travel well and taste good cold. These are by and large suitable for either casual picnics for two or a more formal setting such as Henley where you may be obliged to sing for your supper for some of the MOD's clients. Don't worry – he will be more charming and entertaining than you have ever seen him. He is astute enough to know that his big accounts don't want to hear him boring on about the latest budgetary changes.

Incidentally, I do not include poached salmon in this section because the Dish will *expect* you to make this for the picnic since everyone always does. To borrow the title from Jeanette Winterson's novel, *Oranges are not the only fruit*.

Casual picnics

Why not choose from the following:

1. Asparagus wrapped in Parma ham or smoked salmon	Take a packet of baby wipes for your hands.
2. Potted shrimps	Keep them as cool as possible.
3. Duck breasts with honey and fruit	
4. Unique sandwiches	See below.
5. Cold roast chicken	Roast with lots of garlic, honey, lemon juice, oil and stuffed with the lemon hulls.
6. Cold quiches	Premium supermarket or deli only.
7. Pork pies and cold pork sausages	Make sure you have mustard.
8. Salad	Crunchy and strong coloured things only. Try tying up bunches of cooked green beans with chives.
9. Potato salad	Not shop bought - lazybones.
10. Always have cherry tomatoes, breadsticks, bags of crisps and French bread.	
11. Lemon tart	CookSmart, of course this is one to buy. It is excellent for a hot summer's day. We would urge you to buy the best and most expensive one. 'Maison Blanc' do a good one. The treacherous husband rejected mine for Raymond's!
12. Camembert and blueberries.	

Ambiance	Take a battery operated radio with you and go for Smooth (formerly Jazz) FM.
Dress code	Something accessible.
Conversation	I beg your pardon? Enjoy the tranquillity of the lay by/countryside.

Music

A light background of barely discernable strains of jazz creates something special when you are outdoors. I can almost hear it now.

1. Asparagus

This finger food has several things going for it. It is a sophisticated and unusual way to eat asparagus. What's more, it is versatile – you can wrap it up in different 'blankets' – smoked salmon or whatever kind of ham takes your fancy. We would steer you towards Italian or Spanish rather than English. As for smoked salmon, your predecessors will have just peeled a packet and arranged the fish on a paper plate getting fingers nice and greasy. This is a far more interesting method of presenting it.

2. Potted shrimps

I first experimented with this starter when I was trying to impress Stephen before we were engaged. My mother, as mums do, said I was wasting my time, but *I knew* that it was only a matter of a few more *pièces de résistance* and my patience would be rewarded. I am convinced that this appetiser, which he told me he had eaten a hundred times at 'The Quality Chop House' in Farringdon, helped me land my man.

Don't make the mistake I did. When the fishmonger produced a box of shrivelled *brown* lumps that looked like they had been dragged along a polluted river bed I turned my nose up and went for pink ones. Luckily they tasted great but it turned out that it was the brown little beauties I should have been using.

117

3. Duck breasts with honey, pear and peach halves

My introduction to duck with roast pear cut in an attractive fan shape came via a boyfriend's very nice mother. Nick's mum, Leah, had been, I think, a professional cook at one time and the family owned a house in the south of France. Perhaps this influenced her cooking since I subsequently ate a similar dish, but with roasted peach, in a delightful restaurant in a somnolent hilltop village near Aix en Provence.

Leah made us the duck and delivered it to Nick's home for us to eat after a hard day's work. I liked her – *see* – you can't help feeling positively about someone who has gone to the trouble of making homely and tasty food for you. Pity about her son though. Their part of the Riviera is supposed to be fantastically beautiful and it would have been nice to have checked it out before we split up.

Now that it is coming back to me, I seem to remember Nick saying how lucky he was to find someone who made him oriental-style sea bass mid week! He was quite keen at that point. Never mind, an (ex) best friend who went out with him after me (I recollect she was drying his tears the very next day) had some good dishes up her sleeve too. Cleo's Osso bucco was first rate. I am not sure how extensive her repertoire was. It was a bit of a revolving door in my part of town at the time; he married someone else not long after.

4. Unique sandwiches filled with (1) mountain salami and sliced peeled cucumber (2) Emmenthal cheese and 'Aunt Jessica's' onion marmalade (3) fresh grilled tuna with sliced beef tomato, red pepper, sweet corn and salad cream

What makes sandwiches unique? I wondered this too until, that is, I went to a stylish tea party in northern France hosted by the mother of my enviably chic friend Genevieve. Hanging in the hallway of the apartment was a photograph of a nice but plain schoolgirl. The experience taught me two invaluable lessons. First, that an ordinary brunette can be transformed into a glamour puss by (a) going blonde and having a decent hairdo and (b) applying a shovel full of make up.* Second, that with similar wizardry, the humble sarnie is transformed into a dazzling creation. This is how to do it.

Buy an unsliced loaf. Upend it, *comme ça*, and cut off the 'lid'. Turn the loaf the other way up and repeat, keeping both crusts. Then, with a sharp bread knife, saw the middle out of the loaf, trying to keep as close to the crust as you can. You should end up by removing what looks like an intact loaf. The empty shell becomes an unusual box which you will fill with sandwiches.

Cut the inner 'loaf' into fine slices, butter, and choose your fillings, then re-assemble. First, replace the bottom lid (you only cut this so that it was easier to take out the inside) then pack the sandwiches inside the walls of your box. Between each layer place a piece of baking paper, cut to size, to stop the sandwich layers from welding together. Finally, put back the top lid and wrap the loaf with silver foil to keep it from drying out. When you offer the sandwiches, ask your guest to remove the lid. He will not expect to see sandwiches inside. Impressive or what!

As a postscript to the tale about the French tea party, I would add that Genevieve's mother seemed bizarrely youthful. She swore by the benefits of ice cold showers. I am sorry, but this sort of thing is not for me. I could have kissed the engineer who repaired our broken down boiler today. One freezing shower was plenty, thanks. *And* I became wedged in the baby bath when I tried to have a dip in that using water heated with several kettles. What if the fire brigade had been obliged to rescue me?

5. Cold roast chicken

All I will say here is that the salient point with the chicken is to carve it at the last minute to prevent it drying out. By the way, we might have suggested Coronation Chicken but does anyone actually like it? Apart from Sarah – some people like fruit with meat (i.e. sultanas with chicken) but many men don't.

---

* There is no shame in splashing out once or twice to have a professional make-up artist demonstrate how to apply some slap. French girls know intuitively how to do this. Everyone else may need a guiding hand.

6. Cold quiches

PB's could turn out superior versions but you will have to find a decent shop-bought flan. With so many flavours you may not know which one to choose. Quiche Lorraine is generally a better bet than say, spinach which men associate with Popeye and Olive. Alternatively, you could buy pastry and make the filling but we cannot see the sense of this for a large tart. In our opinion you are either pregnant or you are not. Make it or buy it.

7. Pork pies and cold pork sausages

By now we should not have to tell you what you will need to bring along for these*.

8. Plain smoked salmon

Sorry, another trick to see if you have grasped the direction of this odyssey. No. Too boring.

12. Camembert and blueberries

Take along a few oatcakes/flat breads wrapped in foil to accompany cheese. I happen to think blueberries compliment *fromage*. Strawberries and raspberries disintegrate everywhere so leave them in the fridge to have with a glass of crisp white wine when you return. Apricots and cherries are tasty but then you have to deal with the stones and spitting them out is not a particularly glamorous act.

I have just devoured a sensational snack of chevre from a stall I have not seen before in Chapel Street market in Islington, north London on Sunday. Delish.

Picnic beverages

Alcohol

Because there is a range of food being served, rosé is a pragmatic

---

* okay, if I must. Mustard. In a small plastic pot. And a spoon.

choice. It has a summery touch to it which even white wine does not quite match. Alternatively, for something light in the middle of the day you could do worse than white Sancerre. For an evening affair, opt for white Burgundy.

Coffee
Make proper strong coffee in advance and taste it to make sure it will be good enough for the Dish.

I really began to hit the coffee jar when I started working. To liven up my desk job I would grade coffee when visiting various law firms and barristers' chambers. As a general rule my experience was that the latter served better, stronger brews than the former. They also had superior sandwiches.

Even certain 'magic circle' outfits offered what I considered to be lacklustre coffee – good biscuits though. These firms were printing squillions and could surely afford decent refreshments and I asked myself in those turgid meetings why they didn't. Were they scared of claims of inducing arrhythmia in visitors? Maybe some clever clogs had suggested that the woman in the States who won a shed load of dosh for complaining about hot coffee from McDonald's had set a dangerous precedent which could be extended to visitors who have too much caffeine. Or, had they exhausted the conference room budget on corporate strategists, like *feng shui* experts, who tell you about the yin and yang of pot plants and where to position them to maximise good *chi*? No, my legal brain concludes that no one other than me drinks killer strength coffee.

2. Barbecues

Inspiration : Someone sizzling. We are going to break with tradition and suggest three contemporary glamour dolls - Scarlett Johansson, Kelly Brook and Alesha Dixon – they always look well groomed. We would like to think that neither they, nor you, would '*schloch*' (= mooch) around in shapeless baggy, low slung chinos, camouflage tee and baseball cap for an occasion like this.

Let's turn to more burning issues. I hate to talk about men as if they were stereotypes, but have you ever met a man who doesn't think he is an expert with the coals? You may not like barbecues, but indulge the boy in his primeval love affair. Pander to his thirst for MEAT and fire and he is bound to worship you.

The main event

If you are really observant, you will notice that chicken is omitted from the usual suspects in this carnivorous feast. This is because whenever I see a leg sizzling away on a barbie I do not see meat, only a potential vector of avian flu or salmonella!

Yes, you could accuse me of being unnaturally conscious of food hygiene. It is not that I have poisoned anyone lately. In my defence I would explain that I am a hypochondriac doctor's daughter. I no longer make my favourite dessert of all time, iced coffee soufflé, because it contains raw eggs. Similarly, I am concerned that, if chicken is insufficiently cooked on the flames, someone will get the squits. Never ideal when you are in someone else's home.

In case you were wondering about pre-cooking the meat in the oven, let me dissuade you. As the co-host, you should spend as little time as possible indoors. Furthermore, the taste of the double cooked meat does not appeal to me. For the last time, forget chicken! Make delectable *sauteed* garlic prawns instead. These will be out of the ordinary and therefore more in keeping with your 'signature' style which the Dish is coming to expect of you.

Handy hints to make the occasion run smoothly

Equipment
* Buy extra long matches. Alternatively, watch Ray Mears' survival programmes as he demonstrates how to light a fire with a drawing pin and three blades of dried grass.

- CookSmart followers do not mess around with gas and coals. What a performance! You will be the one having to scour the metal grill. Men probably think that there is no need since bacteria will burn off next time. Ugh. Lay in a stack of disposable barbecues as soon as they appear in the shops since they disappear in a heat wave. If you get ones with built-in stands you need not worry about marking his wretched patio.

- Use tongs to turn meat. Alternatively, watch Ray Mears demonstrate how to fashion a spear from a tree trunk.

Plates and cutlery

If you are in the back garden and have easy access to the kitchen you should eat with real china and use proper glassware. We are not proposing to repeat our views on picnic accoutrements; these principles apply equally to barbecues.

Suggested barbecue foods

1. *Meats with potato salad*	Marinate away!
2. *Potato salad?*	Yes – can be made in advance.
3. *Mediterranean prawns (big fat ones!) in garlic butter*	**Vampire rating 4** Better make sure the MOD is not kosher! Shellfish will be prohibited.
4. *A decent salad*	There are other people present so you must serve something passing for vegetation.
5. *Tabouleh*	Buy lots of herbs.
6. *Chilled 'drunken' cauliflower*	**Vampire rating 4** Another dish which is not run of the mill. This is essentially marinated cauliflower doused in

	sherry vinegar, olive oil, finely chopped garlic, a small tub of stuffed olives (green with pimentos). Cover in clingfilm or your fridge will pong.
7. Duck liver pâté	While the meat and prawns are cooking serve pâté on oatcakes or pieces of toast. I can't write anymore because my mouth is watering.
8. Fresh raspberries	To finish. Simple and classy. Not strawberries. It is broad summer. He will throw up if he sees another one.
Ambiance	A '70's classic – Santana, Pink Floyd or Eric Clapton.
Drink	Lots of cheap red wine. Rough strong wine goes well with these flavours and the guests will not notice.
Dress code	Skimpy and strappy. That is for foot* and shoulder. Pin your hair up? Bold earrings?
Conversation	We doubt you will have much time when you are shuttling between the kitchen and the garden to say more than 'Another glass?'.

* heels on grass doesn't usually work so think *flat* strappy sandals or *low* heels, unless you are sticking to the patio.

1. The usual suspects – steaks – make sure these are first class cuts – best-quality sausages and homemade burgers

Most summers the husband and I plus entourage *schnorrer* (= to visit or stay with people and eat them out of house and home/ overstay welcome by making yourself too much at home in someone else's home) at Paul's house in the New Forest. He and Lauren are gourmands in the sense of being knowledgeable about food rather than greedy. The barbecued Sunday lunch has become a firm ritual.

The lord and master of the household knows how to prepare the best barbecued beef in Hampshire. It is sublimely tender. Paul's secret, to marinate the meat in whisky. Meanwhile, Lauren, a talented chef, chargrills vegetables inside the house – asparagus, baby corn and red peppers. She also makes baked potatoes.

Now I go along with everything they do, but for the life of me, when I chargrill veg on my griddle they come out uncooked inside and burned on the outside. Unless you are competent with your griddle pan I would not therefore attempt this method for a lunch where I *need* to impress. I have just acquired a second griddle pan and I will come back to you if this makes a difference. Check the website: www.thedishbook.co.uk.

2. Baked potatoes or potato salad?

Three good reasons not to have hot spuds in July. 1. We adore baked potatoes but classify them as winter fuel. 2. You always eat later than you expect to by which time the potatoes could resemble grenades. 3. On top of this it is another chore for you to do when your focus needs to be on putting your guests at ease.

I know Sarah and I would make potato salad in advance.

3. Mediterranean prawns (big fat ones!) in garlic butter

I am anxious not to give the impression that in my social circle everyone has a country 'hice' or boat. But, Gabi and Sean, who have a Hansel and Gretl *'chaumiere'* (cottage) in Normandy, lent it to us one freezing Easter. On the only day warm enough to venture outside we made a barbecue, keeping our fingers crossed that we would not set their field on fire. In the morning we bought fresh raw prawns, garlic, butter, duck pâté and raspberries from a local market. These simple ingredients made for the most memorable meal I have ever eaten. You can replicate this.

To cook on the barbecue you will need a frying pan or saucepan which can take the heat of the coals. Melt butter, fry chopped garlic then the prawns. Heavenly.

4. A decent salad

For this occasion we believe that a combination of rocket, cooked baby corn and baby asparagus, served cold, would complement the main event nicely. I do like avocado but it can turn brown when left too long in the open air even if doused in lemon juice.

Or, how about my most recent addition – a brilliant radicchio salad. Soak the leaves in cold water for a few minutes then pat dry. Then, just coat in grated parmesan cheese and throw over a dressing with gumption. Mix up 1 tbsp each of sherry vinegar, balsamic vinegar and Dijon mustard, add some finely chopped garlic, then *slowly* whisk in 2tbs corn oil which you have stirred up with 4 tbs extra virgin oil.

5. Tabouleh

Not entirely dissimilar to cous cous, this is only worth eating if it is prepared with sufficient flavouring. I used to have a great recipe which was on the packet. I wish I hadn't lost it.

SCORE

1. *Commitment*	8	These are proper coupley events.
2. *Romance*	9	You did remember the blanket.
3. *Fun*	8	A good time was had by all.

chapter 11

Sports evenings with the lads

A good cook is like a sorceress who dispenses happiness"
Elsa Schiaparelli (1890-1973) Parisian fashion designer

Inspiration
Sophia Loren! A glimpse of hot stuff is all they will get to see.

The truism that a way to a man's heart is through his stomach applies equally to the MOD's mates. Once you have passed the honeymoon stage in a relationship you must expect a man's attention to revert, partially, to his true love – footie, rugby or God forbid, golf or cricket. And if you are canny you will encourage him to pursue these pastimes solo.

Letting the Dish have the lads around to watch the BIG MATCH is a win-win scenario for you. Firstly, being clingy is unattractive in a woman. This *laissez faire* approach of yours demonstrates your self-confidence. Secondly, you may agree with me that, aside from internationals or big tournaments, watching men chase a ball around a field is excruciatingly tedious.

Admit it. In the same way that we laugh like a drain at a client's poor joke, women feign enthusiasm for some of their boyfriends' interests. Before the ring went on my fourth finger I encouraged *my* intended (I was not *his* intended you see) to buy me the most expensive two tone golf shoes from Harrods so that I could lovingly walk by his side admiring his putting skills during his round at Wentworth Golf Club's three (interminably long) courses. He even paid for me to have a lesson, presuming perhaps that I found it ever so exciting and we would play together for years to come.

Can you guess how often I have played, let alone set foot on a green? *The shoes are in mint condition – yours for £90. Contact me please if you are interested. Size 5.*

So, we would be correct in thinking you will have a more agreeable night if you go out with your friends and leave him to his own devices. There are bound to be dozens of slushy films the MOD will not be taking you to. Lucky for me that Gabi treated me to *The Thomas Crowne Affair* so that I could drool over Pierce Brosnan. My husband refuses to see anything period he calls 'bonnets' or even worse, slushy 'romantic comedies' -anything with the word 'wedding' in the title or featuring Jennifer Aniston. He can be a killjoy.

But, this is where your scheming comes in. You will prepare the most perfect meal for this crowd of armchair athletes that they have ever eaten. You won't *wait* on them, because that would be like having their mums there, asking if they want another cup of tea all the time, when the crucial goals are being scored. Sarah says she did precisely this, when her hubby was watching a game at his prospective best man's house (the girlfriends were gossiping in the kitchen). She breezed in to offer more nuts/crisps/beer and with her curvy derrière blocked the screen just as Giggsy or Gazza was scoring the deciding goal. The boys were incandescent and not in a good way, so she beat a humiliated retreat. So, back to your plan of going out. His friends will think you are fantastic news even if you are only there for five minutes when they arrive.

Here's the plan:- you need to think meat, meat, meat. And beer, beer, beer. There will be no attempt on your part to leave anything which remotely resembles vegetables or fruit. In fact no need to bother with dessert either. And no cutlery – great – men like to eat with their hands!

HAVE LOTS OF NAPKINS FOR GREASY HANDS.

Sporting evening menu

Home made lamb or beef burgers with ketchup in baps	**Vampire rating 2** Think of a number then double it. This has got to be the simplest meat dish to make. Just fry a couple of shallots with garlic then tip into a bowl with chopped rosemary, heaps of black pepper (from a mill) and minced meat. Shape into patties and chill. *Yo man! High five!!*
Crisps and tortilla chips with dips – houmous, sour cream and chives	.
Home-made garlic bread	**Vampire rating 5**
Ambiance	Match of the day.
Drink	Plenty of chilled beer – and remember to put out the opener. Don't bother with glasses.
Dress code	Anything figure hugging. You want the boys to comment on your curves. Acessorised by red lippy.

Conversation	Think you can remember this – 'Nice to meet you. Bye.' Smile your most dazzling smile and flash your beautiful eyes! It doesn't hurt to have the mates think you're gorgeous.

The idea behind this meal is that it is perfect for the cave dwelling carnivore the MOD secretly is. If you don't believe me, then give some thought to what he eats when you are not there. It is unlikely that he would be having the same solitary meal as you.

Good, now that we have a consensus on the issue, let's get down to brass tacks. The beauty of this meal is that you do all the legwork before you leave and even a Neanderthal on his fifth lager could manage to cook it.

Remember what we said about aromatics. You will be tearing up rosemary for the burgers. He already associates this herb with you. Thus you will imprint on his mind an indelible link between football – his sporting passion perhaps - and you. He might even think of you *en passant* but I would not bank on this. It is the 'back handed' praise from the friends that will register with him and it is their goodwill you are really seeking to cultivate with this production.

Garlic bread is another tactic. Please do not cut corners by buying ready-made. It is incredibly simple and quick to make. Just slice a French stick down the middle and smear the cut surfaces with a generous paste made from a couple of cloves of minced garlic and salted butter. Reassemble, wrap in foil and place in the oven for 5-10 minutes.

In his brilliant book *'The Ivy'* AA Gill says burgers should preferably be cooked on a hot barbecue or griddle plate (or a smoking hot cast-iron pan) but not under the grill unless yours is particularly hot since this dries out the meat. I bow to his superior wisdom but all I can say is *'yeah, right, but what do you think we're going to do when the footie's on telly, mate?'*

We do not really hope that either one of us needs to explain to a man how he should cook a burger. He ain't going to spend his time next to the stove when Thierry Henry is about to score.

Tell him to shove the dish in the oven. All he has to do is pull the tray out.

Additional preparations

1.   Leave baps somewhere you think the Dish will be able to find them. Men cannot locate things in fridges – they can only see things if they are *exactly at eye level and straight in front of them.* If the baps are in plastic don't open the bags because they may dry up. Allow 3-4 per person. Put out butter so that the MOD can spread some for the lads. We suspect though that they like their bread served 'commando style' ie butterless.

2.   Have ketchup and mustard on the table.

3.   Leave out the bags of tortilla chips and crisps. It would make the MOD look emasculated if you spooned the dips into bowls.

4.   Just before you leave, place some of the patties on a heat proof dish and the rest on the side near the cooker for seconds, thirds etc.

5.   Put out the garlic bread in foil packages which can be slid onto the bottom part of the oven (or better still in the second part of a double oven if he has one) a few minutes before the burgers are cooked.

6.   Make sure the beer is on ice. Have a couple of bottles of mineral water too just in case someone is driving.

7.   You will not be leaving cutlery but it would be a nice touch to make sure there are tongs for handling the meat.

We have not suggested that you put out a plastic bag for the empties. Men do not do cleaning up. I think you will be Mrs Mop.

SCORE

1. Commitment   8   He will tell you he loves you after this one.

2. Romance   10   His mates are happy and Arsenal won.

3. Fun   8   The chick flick was great.

chapter 12

Casual suppers with the troops

How to win friends and influence people
Dale Carnegie (1888-1955) American writer and
lecturer

Inspiration

Audrey Hepburn – a stylish icon with a happy-go-lucky manner.
Read Truman Capote's excellent *Breakfast at Tiffany's* if you want
to see how the 'real' Holly Golightly came a cropper. Suffice to say
there was no Hollywood ending with beautiful George Peppard.
Study the film for fashion tips.

This is the '*momento pravda.*' You are officially a couple but this is
no time to crack open the champers. The MOD is about to admit
you to his inner circle - and has invited his old college pal and his
long-term girlfriend (who have been living in Oxford) to his place
for a casual supper. There are plenty of banana skins between here
and the church.

The trouble with this scenario, as you probably know, is that established couples – well let's be frank shall we, as it is just you and us – is that the female half is going to lord it over you, because you are a newcomer on the scene. Her boyfriend will probably try and be nice and will get it in the neck afterwards for his trouble. His partner will accuse you of hitting on him.

Before they come, try and find out as much as you can about the couple. This exercise will go more smoothly if you can find some conversational common ground. At the moment you may know precious little about these two other than that they have the power to exclude you if they want. Single women are a threat. If the couple are childless they could spend the entire night reminiscing about uni.

Mean, but that lot are mild compared to what I refer to as the 'barracuda' females with children who (I used to believe) would deliberately turn the talk to the cost of private tutors and Gina Ford's guide to potty training to put you in your place. I have been to cocktail parties where I have stood like a lemon while the mums were enthusing about the merits of Suzuki (I thought this was a motor bike!) versus conventional methods of learning to play a violin. You can't beat them so join them. The truth is that most married women with kids have no conversation beyond the enthralling aspects of being married with kids. You will probably end up as one of them.

What can you say?

It is imperative that you do none of the following.

- Talk about sex.
- Ask what the women do for a living.
- Ridicule their love of pets.
- Discuss the Middle East.

You need to hone in on the topics that most married couples expect to discuss over a meal. They tend to be irrevocably conservative. Insular people are enthralled by planning issues and thrive on neighbourhood disputes. Risqué remarks will be regarded as being in poor taste.

Over the dinner table my husband asked an ostensibly worldly housewife, Meredith, what the secret was to a long marriage and she replied 'having lots of sex' to which he responded by enquiring 'with whom?' I still find his riposte witty but needless to say she did not.

It subsequently transpired that our acquaintance had spearheaded a campaign to have the fascia of a local supermarket *improved* to make it more in keeping with the character of the area. I can't say I noticed anything amiss. I just thought '*great – at last a decent shop*'. Even if I had disliked a shop front – be it a supermarket or a betting shop, it would not in a million years occur to me to round up a pressure group to have it removed. My mindset is just not wired to this frequency.

As for the job situation, leave it to a woman to tell you if she works. The penny has finally dropped that I am the only one to ask another female if she does something remunerative. Perhaps I am the only one who still works. I realise now that the expectation is that most wives do not go down the mine. The last thing they will want is to hear about your interesting career if their other half is present, for fear that they might think that getting them back in the labour market is a good idea! Even in a recession they won't.

Lastly, remember that people are sensitive about their pets and will not appreciate your making them the butt of jokes. Joe (to whose parents I served up the artichoke) has sometimes got a wicked sense of humour. We had a fondue once at the home of his best friend, Brendan and his vivacious missus, Samantha. Our hostess was very attached to a cute small, hairy dog that accompanied her everywhere. There was even a photograph of the doggie on the bookshelf. While she was out of the room my mischievous friend whisked the photo down and propped it up on the dinner table in front of the meat for the fondue as if to say '*look what we are having for dinner!*' Again I was paralysed with giggles but I seem to remember the lady of the house was not.

But, it is absolutely vital that you get on with these strangers because they are clearly important to him. Men tend to be influenced by their close friends who can get unnecessarily territorial. The priority is to make them feel welcome and not threatened by your presence. What could achieve this humble aim better than a decent meal?

Having just returned from the sun a while back on a local airline which served us a dull 'cattle class' meal, I was astonished to have a virtual carbon copy dinner at a supper party. This was an appalling demonstration of overcooked slop. We are very clearly trying to help you avoid replicating this meal.

We now sniggeringly refer to all food catered in this *maison* as 'doors to manual' meals. You only know you are on the ground because there are plates, not compartmentalised trays. For dinner it might be either dried-up '80's bistro salad (ie goats cheese on limp lettuce and forgettable salad dressing) followed by chicken or beef (close your eyes and imagine an air hostess offering you this choice and you know what unappetising fare we get) – consistently overcooked and smothered in a glutinous sauce. Even roast potatoes, I suspect, are microwaved from the deep freeze. I wish you could have witnessed the poor cook hyperventilating over a roast one lunch time. Her husband tried to placate a mob of hungry guests armed only with fifth rate supermarket canapés. I had lost my appetite for the meal by the time it eventually arrived. 0/10.

You learn with experience that with some people you need to have a substantial snack before you leave home.

Another couple unfailingly get it right. The missus, Diana, researches Italian history, possibly as a cover for her frequent trips to the country to pick up culinary tips – and lovely clothes. Her cooking style is brisk and efficient, the cuisine based on simple, punchy 'attitude' dishes. Cabbage and chestnut soup, baked good-quality sea bass with leeks. Excellent cheeses. Best of all, coffee made in a Bialetti. I look forward to visiting them. 10/10.

In many ways you will find that it is more difficult to decide what is appropriate for someone else's friends than any other category of guest because what is served must be neither too fancy nor too plain. The idea to convey here is that you have gone to some trouble without over-egging the pudding. This says you are confident of your position but are not trying to isolate him from his past.

A pretentious meal such as venison with a complicated sauce and wild *girolles* mushrooms sautéed in truffle oil followed by a choice of six elaborate desserts would backfire. Straightforward flavoursome cuisine is what is needed.

Over confidence can be a bad thing but, do not worry your pretty little head over this encounter. We have navigated your path skilfully so far. Now, leave everything to us. We have, as always, cherry-picked a selection of sublime dishes and, to get matters off to a flying start, the time is ripe to bring out our culinary big gun – THE HONEY LEMON ROAST CHICKEN! Eat this and weep boys!

PS. If your kitchen and dining rooms are on different levels I would rethink your eating arrangements. Carting laden trays up and down a narrow staircase invites disaster.

Menu 1

| La specialité de ma maison *(AKA honey lemon roast chicken) with roast potatoes and broccoli* | **Vampire rating 3**
The key to delectable roast chicken is to make incisions in the skin and stuff them with garlic, then to stuff the inside with more garlic and 2 lemon halves having squeezed over the juice first. Douse with honey and oil and baste occasionally.

Organic chicks can sometimes be tough so choose carefully from a butcher you trust. |

Carrot halwa	What in heaven's name is this? It is an Indian curiosity, that's what it is. A sort of cardamom-infused cross between a sweetmeat and a compote. Sometimes you need to make something which no one has eaten before.
Ambiance	Easy listening – Elton John or The Eagles.
Dress code	Demure – a soft palette please rather than a harsh monochrome or vivid splashes of colour. Large ethnic beads and bangles? Yes, good. Note please that drawstring trousers are unflattering on the botty unless you are skinny. If you are skinny, then lord it! Casual chic is the effect to create here.
Drink	On this occasion let him choose. After all, they are his friends.
Any other points?	Have you got a bright tablecloth?
Theatre	These two are cultured. Get hold of some brochures from your local theatre, and read them. It may come in handy later tonight.

Carrot Halwa

Everyone I know who has set foot over the threshold has been subjected to this treat. I came across it in someone else's newspaper one day and carefully excised it for my scrap book. (PB that I am!).

If you are going to sustain your foodie campaign it is a good idea to scour recipe pages of mags, newspapers, freebie estate agents magazines etc for recipes and cut them out. Put them in a box somewhere the Dish won't find them. We would like to reassure you ladies that neither of us belong to the group of women who remove pages from Cosmopolitan at the hairdressers.

I have over the years adapted the recipe so that it is now, in my opinion, perfect. Although my version is a closely guarded secret, since I now consider you to be a friend, I will let you have it.

Carrot Halwa
Ingredients
80g caster sugar
60g butter plus a spoonful for cooking raisins
3 tbs raisins
300g carrots, peeled and grated
10 cardamom pods, bashed
lemon juice
200 ml semi skimmed milk

Method
Melt a large dollop of butter in a saucepan and cook the raisins for a couple of minutes. Drain the butter and reserve the fruit. Heat the remaining butter (60g ish) in a large frying pan, add the carrot and cook, stirring continuously for 5 mins. Add the milk, and pods, boil briefly, then reduce the heat and cook over a gentle heat for 10 mins. Spoon over the sugar and continue to cook until the mixture has become nicely glutinous. Carefully remove the pods and throw away. Sprinkle over the raisins and finally adorn with a dash of lemon juice. Chill. Pile into individual ramekins if you wish.

Menu 2

Roast marinated lamb with cubed garlicky roast potatoes and mangetout.	**Vampire rating 3** A CookSmart favourite method of preparing meat is to leave it overnight in a dry bath of strongly-flavoured bits and bobs – chillies, garlic, lemon juice, lemon rind, ginger, cumin, onion, dried apricots and oil. This process tenderises the meat as well as gives it punch.

	Warning!! Fire alarm – if you are cutting chillies for your marinade use a knife and fork or rubber gloves to handle them otherwise you could scorch someone when you touch them!
Crème renversée à l'orange	A posh name for orange flavoured *crème caramel*. Only make this if you have individual ramekins or similar heat resistant dishes. Unless you are a miracle worker, if you make it in a large bowl, it will never set. For this dish you will only need the grated orange zest. So, to make the evening ahead a more pleasant prospect, squeeze the orange juice and drink it while cooking, mixed with Vodka. We would serve this dessert with sliced oranges doused in loads of cointreau. Might as well make use of the MOD's booze. Garnish with a couple of strategically-placed mint leaves. Whoops, you can't do this if you have used up the oranges for your aperitif. Recall your 'O'level/GCSE physics? Water is a conductor of heat. So, if your oven gloves have become wet during cooking, dry them before you use them again! *We do not, repeat do not, want to have this book hijacked by you into becoming a cookery book. Go out and buy one. There are millions to choose from. Personally I would go for all of Robert Carrier's. I am also a fan of Gordon's.

	So, you can't find *crème renversee* anywhere! And I let you have the carrot halwa. I suppose I could see this coming. OK, for the last time. I will let you have the recipe for this too. No more. See below. And don't tell Sarah.
Drink	Husband is the wine buff and is tiring. As is probably obvious to you, I can barely distinguish between red and white. Fortunately, by making the right marriage I have bought into some seriously boring, but necessary (for this book) knowledge. I (he) would suggest a red Cotes du Rhone.
Ambiance	Will Young, Amy Winehouse; cool, crowd-pleasers.
Dress	Take your chances. Look 'with it' tonight in case the MOD thinks you are turning into a frump. Black well-cut trousers, black tee shirt, silver sandals. Go easy on the make up though.

Recipe for Crème Renversée à l'Orange
Ingredients
250 ml milk
grated zest of 2 oranges
100g caster sugar
2 eggs
2 egg yolks

Method: Heat the orange zest with the milk and 50g sugar to boiling point. Remove, cover the pan and leave to infuse for half an hour. Whisk the eggs and yolks and then decant through a sieve over the milk.

Cover the remaining sugar in a saucepan with a minimum of water and heat until it turns to caramel then divide between the ramekins (depending on size you may have a spare crème caramel or two for you to eat surreptitiously at midnight!). Ladle in the egg mixture then place in a bain marie in the oven at 150 degrees until it cracks in the centre. The term bain in this context just denotes a deep ovenproof dish which you fill with water so that it comes three quarters of the way up the sides of the ramekins. I put in a bit of water before I place it in the oven and then top up once it is in the oven using a long spouted kettle and wearing protective oven gloves.

Once cooked allow to cool and chill until suppertime. Invert onto little plates. I use a grapefruit knife to loosen the edges before turning the ramekins over.

Potatoes
You have already done ordinary roast potatoes with the chicken so you cannot make them again for a while. Remember that Cook Smart principles dictate that *'variety is the spice of life'*.

I first tried cubed roasties at a small family run *pension* in the South of France, *L'Hotel de la Plage* in La Faviere. They would serve them for Sunday lunch with roast *poussin*. Not alas somewhere *tres luxe*, in the hills above Cannes but, to say it was more Dover than Deauville, would be unfair. This is the real Bourgeois France and the local beaches rival anything in the Caribbean.

When I first stayed at this charming Provencal hotel I was only seven and vineyards surrounded it. Alas, the vines are a distant memory buried under shops and flats. But, on the positive side, the place is still operated by the same welcoming family and the prices seem to be frozen at 1970's rates. I don't quite know how they do it but the food remains world class. *Magret de canard*, roast lamb and *rascasse* (white fish) are served with an aplomb which would humble a top London chef.

It is possible that I became hooked on caffeine at this tender age because my parents treated me to an ice cream sundae known as a *café liegois* every day for two weeks. I certainly became as podgy as a freshly baked *pain au chocolat*, a local *specialité*. Thanks for your concern, I'm a size 10 now.

Now that a budget airline flies to the tiny Hyeres airport – not twenty minutes from the hotel – this makes an ideal location for a weekend 'grand gesture' which won't break the bank. See more in Chapter 15. The MOD will be impressed that you appreciate the idiosyncratic style and charm that small hotels can provide *and* take on board that you have not simply elected for 'the large five star hotel' which can at times be anonymous. By all means if the MOD is picking up the tab (and money is no object) don't hang back – go for the Byblos near St Trop darling. After all, it is important to show too that you are not intimidated by glitz even if you are renting a one bed flat in Doncaster.

Menu 3

Borlotti beans with fried pancetta and cheese accompanied by a salad of ruccola aka radicchio? (reddish salad leaves) and vine tomatoes with balsamic vinegar	**Vampire rating 2** Another CookSmart special this. It really doesn't matter how much garlic, pancetta, tomato, cheese and spinach you throw into this dish. Just pop in the oven. Yum! The texture of dried, then soaked, beans is infinitely better than tinned ones but you don't want to be caught with a bowl of soaking water do you? This is pure plum bottling. So use tins.
Grilled or baked peaches with crème fraiche	Or mascapone with sugar. Or vanilla ice cream. You choose. When you are hitched make baked ricotta which is sublime.
Drink	Astura Nazzuro, Nastura Azzura ?– you know which one we mean.

Ambiance	Three Tenors.
Dress	Something wildly unsuitable. You deserve a break. Make it short, tight and loud. Slapper shoes. Fishnets. Red lipstick.

Dress

We would not be surprised if you ignore our suggestion and plump for something elegant – monochrome perhaps. Good. A chic look.

Everyone makes fashion mistakes. My most glaring one was a thigh skimming canary yellow stretchy dress. What was I thinking of when I bought it? I realised it was wrong when I went to a party in one of those substantial mansion flats next to the Albert Hall and was concerned to notice my boyfriend sizing up a striking Italian girl wearing a sophisticated black lace dress. A warning bell sounded. I never wore the banana skin again.

Sarah begs me not to get her started on fashion mistakes – she claims to have bought so many tops which she feels are barmaidy - but she still keeps on buying them. Leopard print, tight lycra, low-cut, clingy – and that was on her wedding day! Boom Boom!

Food

You will have noticed that we are crossing to *Italia*. In keeping with the continental theme we have suggested an Italian lager which needs to be properly chilled. If you don't drink beer, like Sarah, who has never even tasted a sip, because "it smells like sweat" go for the Nasturro Asti thing.

Borlotti beans

I first came across dried borlotti beans in a covered market in Rimini. They looked enticing, all red and shiny. I could not resist buying a large packet to take home.

Rummaging in food markets with a boyfriend can be hugely

enjoyable. Take the Dish to one stocked with delectable goodies when you are on holiday (or at home) and he may begin to imagine what you would do with all those wonderful ingredients. That's the train of thought you need to encourage.

I'll bet he buys you something for the kitchen. Now, in my courting days (don't be insolent, I am not talking about the 1800's) when my husband offered to treat me to some Alessi scales in Milan I unwisely said that I did not want them *until* we were engaged. But I should have realised that the selection of this type of gift is a prelude to the bended knee. Otherwise he would have just been giving me the usual non-committal garbage a man offloads on you after a business trip– perfume, lingerie, scarves and chocolates. I have a collection of unwanted and tasteless items from various duty-free shopping sprees. I am not very grateful.

I like to return gifts – to the shop mind you, not the donor. Tiffany kindly let me exchange a scarf bought in New York by Nick even without a receipt. So, instead of a gift chosen by him in the city that never sleeps, I now have a rather lovely silver necklace and matching bracelet. *Ta.*

Menu 4

Asparagus Risotto accompanied by a warm salad of courgette and tomato	**Vampire rating 2**
Pannetone bread and butter pudding	Use a mixture of cream or crème fraiche and milk to give a smoother texture.
Drink	Elderberry wine.
Dress	Cream ruffled collared blouse and long tweed skirt, a green gilet.
Ambiance	Barry Manilow.

Come off it! Do you seriously think you are going to make this? No one in their right minds makes risotto for four people two of whom they don't really know. My husband (what can I say?) made this dish on our first dinner date. Invited for dinner I expected to see only him. There was a roomful of family and friends including a (delightful) childhood chum of Stephen's who had once taken me out for a disastrous date. Now here he was with new girlfriend. Great.

And mine host made risotto! I did not get to speak to him until the second course because he was fussing over the bubbling rice.

Risotto is *banned* from this book (although you can make it for just the two of you) because, to make it properly, it must absorb large quantities of white wine and stock at regular intervals. This can take 20 odd minutes when you should be attending to your guests. However, as Sarah reminds me, Delia does have a recipe for oven-baked wild mushroom risotto, which gets round this exact problem. It's made creamy with evaporated milk, sherry and Parmesan and is lovely! I should really test drive it.

As for the pud, well this is fabulous but a bit too Mary Poppins – needs a nursemaid to check on progress periodically. So, nope.

Genuine Menu 4

Mustard and dill chicken with rice and green beans	**Vampire rating 2** Mustard sauce is just made by adding a couple of tbsp of Dijon mustard plus some chicken stock to the saucepan in which you have fried the chicken. I also throw in some dill during cooking as well as after to maximise the taste.
Marrons a la Crème	A sophisticated blend of chestnut *purée* and sugar with *crème fraiche*.

	Your grandma may recall this old fashioned number. Dissolve a cupful of sugar in some tinned *purée* which you have heated gently. Cool and lightly mix in some *crème fraiche* and adorn with honey and if you can be bothered, some white chocolate buttons.
Drink	White Sancerre.
Ambiance	Something stylish – Lenny Kravitz
Dress	Palazzo pants and tight top, if your tum can take it. Discrete earrings.

Now, this will be a tasty meal and uses flavours that you have not cooked with much before. The dessert is quite esoteric and comes from the 1940's apparently. Sounds like it's right up your street for a polished supper with the Dish's one pair of hugely glamorous, high flying friends.

It is, I suppose, a reflection of the level playing field in our society that we probably all know a few people who have risen to meteoric heights, as opposed to rising without trace.

There is a famous Russian proverb which says that *'there is no greater joy in life than seeing your best friend fall from the roof'*. You have to be made of strong stuff not to be jealous. My husband manages to be glad for other people. I am just green. Insanely. The couple that spring to mind for me are both six foot tall, outrageously handsome and unbelievably nice. Sydeny has a fantastically glamorous job and Arvin's a city whiz kid. They are polished and rich and live in a beautiful house with staff. I've only seen it in a magazine. But, are they happy?

What kind of twit are you?

Menu 5

Lasagne with fresh peas or broad beans (from the pod, yes they do come from pods not green packets in the frozen foods section)	**Vampire rating 2** Fresh beans/peas taste good if you can be bothered to shell them. See if you can borrow a small child to do this. This is the sort of repetitive mind-numbingly boring task they like to do.
Rum and raisin ice cream/chocolate ice cream	
Drink	Lager or wine for the beer virgins?
Ambiance	Sugar Babes- do you want the girl to look bored?
Dress	Your female guest will make you feel ancient. Respond to her teenybopper style with sophistication. Go for something cream and slim-fitting with high heeled sandals. Consider investing in a blow dry.

This meal is perfect for the MOD's good chum with a new younger girlfriend barely out of nappies. You will be wary about serving food which is over elaborate because you do not want to be responsible for frightening the poor lamb away. This dish will appeal to all ages.

Dress
What you wear is going to be a bit tricky this time. Normally you know we would say that you do not want to make your female guests feel out of place. On this occasion this consideration does not apply since it is unlikely that this girlfriend will be around for too long and she could be too wrapped up in herself, as young things are, to dress in a way which does not make *you* feel

awkward. What you want to avoid here is the Dish wondering if his chum has got a better deal by having a much younger model in tow.

Joe still has an 'other half' who is half his age. When they met he delighted in saying she was 21, he 'double 21.' The girl in question turns out to be an accomplished cook who makes exemplary duck. At first, my husband admitted to being jealous of his contemporary having made such a youthful conquest. However, he has not as yet – I think – tried to get one himself. I am thanking *White v White* (a leading divorce case). He knows that by the time I have finished with him he would not be able to afford to take a date anywhere but McDonald's.

Smoking
Which reminds me about guests who smoke. I have three regular guests who chain smoke. Well, two and an in-law. When they come for supper, much like small children fidget, they are incapable of sitting throughout the meal without lighting up. What do you do? You must tell them it's ok to leave the table for a few minutes and let them smoke outside in the garden/car/street.

Ice cream
Buy decent quality shop bought. If you know the MOD has a penchant for strawberry fondant ice cream from some obscure shop go there if it is conveniently located, but do not go specially to the other side of town to buy it.

PS A note about ready made ices.
I am pretty sure that all commercially made ice cream is churned in the same vast factory just outside Northampton as I have never been able to distinguish between the brands. So, it will be time perhaps for a little white lie and tell him you have managed to track down his favourite kind.

PPS what if you suddenly find out the friends are vegetarian?
How about a cheese fondue?

Cheese fondue   **Vampire rating 3**

Make sure you have some meths. This is particularly hard to find after 5.30pm on a Saturday afternoon. My last fondue was nearly aborted when I could not locate our old bottle of methelated spirit for the burner. Could this finally be the explanation for the mystery as to how a builder managed to get a bonfire going so well on a rainy day? Needless to say this highly combustible fuel was not on sale in Sainsbury's and supper was only rescued because our old next door neighbours were Swiss.

New to the area and working all day I had not had much opportunity to engage in more than rushed conversation with the couple in the next house until that evening – we exchanged pleasantries in the street, and because I overheard them speaking German in the garden, that is what I assumed them to be. But, Heidi and Jorges established Helvetian credentials by virtue of the fact (a) that the interior of their house had lots of wood and a cuckoo clock (b) they *had* meths and (c) they were impeccably polite.

Other than ensuring that you have the correct proportions of cheese there is very little here which can go wrong.

SCORE

1. Commitment	7	Another box ticked.
2. Romance	3	You are probably bored senseless by his friends.
3. Fun	1	Endured.

chapter 13

Power dinner parties

"The guests are met, the feast is set:
May'st hear the merry din"
The Rime of the Ancient Mariner
Samuel Taylor Coleridge (1772-1834) English poet
and philosopher

Inspiration

What better role model than Jacky O? The girl done good. A status
wife to two of the world's most powerful men, JFK and Aristotle
Onassis. Alternatively, Michele Obama. She has first lady style
aplenty. Take heed: she apparently makes a mean seafood gumbo.

Now, this should be interesting. The MOD is sufficiently impressed
with you and/or your entertaining skills (award yourself a gold star
for effort, presentation and content and celebrate on your own with
bought fish and chips, mushy peas and a fantastic lager) to ask you
to co-host a proper dinner party one Saturday in June. But, hang
on, it is only April.

Here are the clues to recognising that this is supposed to be a *'power'* dinner:

- He has pored over lists of invitees for days
- He has invited the Chosen Ones *two* months ahead of the event - IMPORTANT PEOPLE either are really, really busy or - pretend they are and
- There could be work implications if he has asked a colleague or even the boss and his lovely wife.

Needless to say, you are expected to turn in a stellar performance. This might at last present itself as a daunting experience.

I can vouch for the fact that business entertaining at home will be appreciated by the Dish. I often prepare supper for my husband's out of town customers. Of late I have met charming Mr Sohn from Korea, a serious non-English speaking Russian from Otz and Plotsk (ie I haven't got a clue where he hailed from since he could not even manage hello) and the delightful Vadim and Dimitry. What luck that I had been watching *Anastassia* (my daughter's Russian fairytale DVD) that very day and the hero is called Dimitry!

Not only does wheeling out food at home save on restaurant bills (the MOD will appreciate your thrift - keep a tally of what you have saved his business then, at some convenient point, you have the bargaining chip to persuade him to spend it on a fabulous outfit for you) but also it is patently obvious that homesick travellers are grateful to have a home-cooked meal in convivial surroundings. A welcome change from nondescript hotel/restaurant food. Vadim sent a charming e-mail thank you and my husband clinched a mega deal with him that will catapult his company into the FTSE 100 too. Well, not really. It just helped keep the bailiffs away for a few more months.

As these types of guests are important to the MOD, for the first time in your relationship, you will find he has a genuine interest in the arrangements. So you will need to sit him down with a glass of wine and let him get it off his hairy chest. This might be a good time to sit at his feet. Men like that. Take a piece of paper and affect a secretarial manner, taking down his every word. As soon as he has finished and left the room, discard it, since he has absolutely NO idea what he is talking about.

Sarah adopts a similar tactic. She says Peter takes no interest in the menus she is planning until the day, in fact the *hour* before the meal. Then he starts panicking like a headless chicken – have they got enough vegetables? Do they need broccoli? Shall she go to the shop and get broccoli? Has she got cheese from the artisan cheese maker? (no, they've got organic British cheeses from the supermarket – how bad can they be?) She used to listen to him and reason with him. Now she just raises her eyebrows calmly and says, she's doing the food, he's doing the wines, no-one will leave hungry.

Remember, power dinners are meat and drink to the sophisticated lady that you are fast becoming by reading this book.

But, before we get to the meat and drink part we are going to raise a couple of important points about your big evening.

Men whose name begin with C

First do you mind if I ask if the MOD's name begins with a C? It is just that I have found that some men whose name starts with this letter of the alphabet seem to have a mental block about keeping the central heating turned on, even when it is minus 14 outside. Part of keeping your guests happy is to maintain your home at an ambient temperature.

My (I admit rather odd) theory about temperature control began when I met my husband (minus his silly Santa disguise) at a country house weekend party in the shires hosted by a pleasant fellow whose name began with this letter. Let's call him Crispin. A fitting name since it makes me think of chilly weather. His jolly circle of chums were seriously into hunting, shooting and fishin'. In fact, a lot of the people in that set had abbreviated names/nicknames, some based

153

on their surnames. So, if your last name was Knight the chances are you would be called 'Good'. Ha ha!

The idea was for the crowd to watch/participate in a fox hunt in the morning, then in the evening go on to a hunt ball at a splendid house nearby. I was most definitely not into chasing Basil Brush and my interest in foxes is limited to a nice pretty stole. But, all the same, I suppose it was a *faux pas* for me to make my appearance after *la chasse* was over, preferring to be tucked up in bed at home in the metropolis with Vogue on a chilly November morning, than to set off at 5am to stand by some frozen field watching the chase. It was also bitter that night and I resorted to sleeping in my mother's borrowed mink jacket, a 1920's touch to my evening attire.

It was a homely skill which led to Stephen noticing me. Early in the evening I volunteered to repair his torn DJ. As well as making great *confiture,* Grandma Kitty was a seamstress, and I too, am a wizard with needle and thread. A year or so later we had dinner at Crispin's London home where he and Arabella's radiators were stone cold in late November despite a thick frost on the ground. I wore a short sleeved *devoré* number. To cap it all, his 40th was in a marquee on a freezing summer evening. With hindsight, I don't think that teaming my long dress with wellies, was a good look. Now, although I am fond of this couple I would only see them in broad summer.

Dress to impress

Let us start on this occasion with what you are going to wear. Both Sarah and I are keen observers of the image projected by 'power wives' at important dinner parties. Clothes are an essential element of this. How about a deliciously daring *Max & Co* slinky, low-cut black halterneck dress slit above the knee worn with high wattage perfume and winklepickers? A good 'results' look when you are scanning for boyfriend material at a drinks do but totally wrong for a serious dinner party hostess. Why? I should know as I have this frock. It would (does) alienate most female guests at twenty paces. They will (1) be unhappy about their partners' interest in your cleavage and (2) be made more conscious of not having shed the remaining 5 kilos after childbirth. Their youngest is probably six now.

The wives of powerful men know that it is inappropriate to dress to thrill on occasions like this. They uniformly opt for one of two styles. There is the monied, slightly matronly chic approach (lots of Missoni knitwear or a black Chanel cocktail dress accessorised with a modern long string of pearls – short ones are too grannyish and an obvious hand me down). Then there is the jeans and a crisp white colourless blouse look. The idea of the second style is to appear utterly self-assured – the women that opt for this kind of attire know that their guests will be wearing their best dresses and the hostess is demonstrating how unaffected she is by her grandeur.

Conclusion: fit in with, not outshine your guests. Work JFK's bride's demure style to death and you will not go far wrong. A LBD (little black dress) would be just the ticket. The best thing about black is that a stylish inexpensive black number usually holds its own against a designer version. To prove the point, I have a £30 strapless Mango column dress (cunningly altered in one hour by my own fair hand to almost replicate the dress the long lost Anastassia wears to the ballet in Paris in the Fox Family Films DVD!). It looks a million dollars.

Ambiance

Obvious – go classical – any Mozart symphony, but low key as people need to be able to hear.

Conversation

The thought of making small talk or engaging the person sitting next to you in more serious conversation could be scary. But it is actually going to be *incredibly* easy. We guarantee you that there is one subject that will succeed with all of the guests. Their favourite topic – THEM. It is going to be a me, me, me fest. Most people are fascinated by themselves, more so if they are successful. If you probe gently into their life and business coups they will be difficult to turn off. Do not expect a single enquiry about yourself. I have given a name to this type of arrogant self-absorbed behaviour in homage to a particularly self-congratulatory creep I used to know. No I am not going to disclose his identity.

Additional remarks

Setting

Now is the time to pull out the stops on dressing the table. Ideally, get this out of the way the day before the party. You have my permission to bring out the candles *at last*. Use either a white or cream tablecloth and matching napkins. My restaurateur friend, Lauren, impressed upon me the wow effect of folding napkins dramatically.

Have side plates for bread but no one will eat butter so there is no need to agonise over where to place a butter knife. *OK*, I assumed you knew – side plates go on the left.

I know it is fashionable to use oil instead of butter, but really this is not a good idea. The MOD's career will go into nosedive if the boss' wife gets oil on her silk Pucci print smock. *I* ruined a lovely pink chiffon number a few weeks ago when a splodge of oil spattered my dress at a restaurant. Stephen said I should put tonic water on the stain. The local dry cleaners confirm this is an old wives' tale and it just leaves a water mark. So, if you see someone with a dusty pink dress and a large black flower pinned to the bosom you know it is me.

Glassware

I am afraid that Marigolds will be used a lot tonight. You will need three sets of glasses;- for pre-dinner drinks, wine glasses on the table and water glasses on the side. Don't forget to put plenty of Perrier in the fridge.

Drinks

Which brings me onto the subject of booze. Follow my advice explicitly. Forget what we told you about not buying bubbly until the engagement. This is different. An *investment*. First, he will be paying for the shopping. Second, this is not for the two of you but for the benefit of his guests.

As an aperitif, no other beverage sets the tone for an event quite like champagne. It announces that the occasion is smart and special and creates the expectation that the meal will be fun. Any of the following will be magnificent – *Moet & Chandon, Canard Duchene or Tattinger.*

For dinner, you will need to serve a white for the first course, a good red for the main and dessert. Interestingly, there seems to have been a return to the postprandial drink – port or brandy even. If you have them and no one is driving, then why not suggest a *digestif?*

Tit bits

Are nibbles before dinner compulsory? On balance we would answer this in the affirmative because some people will be starving and others (like me) adore salty eats. Avoid crisps or Pringles (not classy enough) and olives (oil stains again). Good *canapés* are all very well but then no one will have room for supper. Really, the only options left will be Japanese rice crackers and those dried tropical fruit mixes which come with strips of dried coconut. The cook (me) has a propensity to remove the coconut and eat it. Someone will notice.

Choice of dishes

You need to serve food that does not need a chaperone.

Because there are three courses you will notice that I have selected *hors d'oeuvres* which can be prepared either in advance or extremely easily, mains that won't dry out if the timing of your event goes haywire, and cold desserts.

CookSmart tip: Someone is invariably late, generally the couple who have the shortest distance to travel. Efficient planners therefore avoid roasts that could become incinerated or fish like tuna where timing is critical to success. Linger over your inter-course chit chat one minute too long and you will find eight pieces of shoe leather in the oven.

Do you need staff?

You are supposed to be showing off how well you can cope, so certainly not. If you like the idea of having a kitchen helper or a team of cooks, when you are safely married is the time to reveal your opinion that domestic assistance is more in keeping with your status.

Timing

A nice interval is needed between courses. About 5-15minutes depending on whether you are followed into the kitchen by the other ladies. This is not speed eating, but neither must guests wonder if they will ever be fed.

Remember too that you are not here to relax. Load dishes as you go along if you are out of sight of your guests, and have a dishwasher tab already in the machine so it can finish its first cycle by dessert. If there are things which can only be hand washed it is a good idea to have a washing up bowl and tea towels at the ready.

However, if you are eating in an open-plan home, the drone of the dishwasher can distract. In that case, leave all washing up to the end. It makes guests feel guilty that they should offer to help. The work of a dinner party should be invisible – it should be done beforehand à la CookSmart, and look effortless on the night.

Then, with luck you should be able to clear up everything else afterwards without too much trouble. The first thing your beau must see next morning is nothing - out of the ordinary that is – and he will not since you DO NOT GO TO BED before everything is in apple pie order. NB take the rubbish out. And take them *right* to the bins, otherwise the foxes will get them. Black bin liners are neither a fetching sight or smell the morning after the night before. It's a bit like seeing remnants of old make up you cannot be bothered to remove.

The MOD's role

A bit of acting is required here to make him think he is the architect of this fabulous extravaganza. You could, I suppose ask him to open the bottles so that he takes credit for the bacchanalian compliments. He is also the one who should be taking coats and *hanging* them up. Clear a space for outer garments to go and make sure the Dish knows where this is.

Food

Without further ado this is what you need to make. Note that three courses are *de rigeur*.

Menu 1

Terrine d'Aubergine and tomate	**Vampire rating 2** In plain English, fried aubergine slices topped with a peppery, garlicky tomato sauce made by simmering together some chopped and skinned tomato with oodles of black pepper, some garlic and a little sugar. Grate over with parmesan.
Coq au vin with mange touts, green beans and rice	**Vampire rating 2** I am convinced that it is utter tosh what quality of wine you use for cooking. This is tastiest if made the day before your extravaganza.

Sherry trifle	Men adore proper English puddings like this or hot desserts such as bread and butter pudding. But a CookSmart chef would not make any dessert for a formal party which requires either her presence in the kitchen (eg zabaglione) or only so much cooking time in the oven. It is ok to finish something off like a tart which needs to have the top caramelised but note that the melting sugar can trigger the smoke detectors. Mustn't have the guests thinking they are about to be *flambéed*.
Drink	St Julien (remember, top class Claret)
Any other points	Do a table plan this time. It is more fun to separate couples. Try not to seat the married man the MOD most wants to impress next to a single blonde/single brunette/single anything that moves. Married women see a bit of Charlie in any unattached female.

Starter – aubergine and tomato layers

This ought to start things off very smoothly. You will I hope be grateful to us for the fact that this is something you can largely make in advance and pop in the freezer.

In this *hors d'oeuvre* I simulated a fabulous starter eaten on a rickety table outside in the street at the smallest pizza/pasta restaurant in Cassis, a pretty port near Marseilles. In olden days it was famous for its fishing boats and *les calanques* – the creeks. More recently (thanks to my warnings) it can be associated with nimble footed thieves who break into your top floor hotel bedroom in dead of night. Tip: If you are staying in a hotel in a hot climate put the air con on at night and secure the shutters, or alternatively, go out with (or marry) a marine or commando who can take care of himself in this sort of situation.

Coq au vin

I adore this. It encapsulates the magic of French cuisine. Eat this and your dinner guests will conjure up a vision of the archetypal dark, mirrored and brass countered Parisian bistro they have been to – probably with someone other than their current partner.

I confess that I made this casserole recently for my uncle's 70th birthday dinner but unfortunately ran into a spot of bother.

My other half was away. I raided the drinks cupboard and took two red St Julien 1984 (I assume that any bottle left in my domain was approved for cooking purposes) and damn it, the corks were stuck. Claiming this was an emergency, I persuaded my neighbour Sasha to send over her husband Jolyon. He is one of those capable sorts who has jump leads, opens wine for hopeless ladies in distress and probably regrets living near us. He appeared a bit offended. Jolyon intimated that it was sacrilegious to use THIS wine for cooking. Was I sure I knew what I was doing? I don't like red wine and, so far as I am concerned, cooking is the only fit use for it. However, to err on the side of caution (and he *was* right about my not knowing what I was doing) I did not use the wine. *Rot. OF course I did. I had eight people coming for dinner the next day.*

The Cognac is one ingredient not to get carried away by. If you take a punt at how much you are using and, by accident, pour in too much you could end up with a mini inferno! Twice now I have had to slam the lid over the casserole to cut off the oxygen supply and turn off the heat in order to extinguish energetic flames. If you panic at this juncture and forget to use oven gloves you might get a nasty burn from the lid since the casserole will have been in the oven already. I learned this the hard way too.

There is an optimum level of alcohol in a recipe – more is not better. Sarah remembers doing fresh pineapple macerated in Malibu (it was the 90s). Whooh! It was potent – people couldn't really eat it.

Sherry trifle

I went to a friend's mother's worthy charity event. As I was leaving, I was so impressed with the dessert that, on impulse, I recommended to a complete stranger who was just coming into the room, that she should try the trifle. It transpired she had made it – and she very kindly sent me a recipe which she said was from Katie Stewart. I am sorry but I don't know who she is. I have heard of the former jailbird, Martha Stewart.

Sarah does know who Katie was. She thinks she used to do a cookery column in The Times. Where is she now?

Menu 2

Salad of feta cheese, watercress and spinach with orange	
Lamb tagine with cous cous and minted carrots	**Vampire rating 4** You really need a *Le Creuset* casserole dish on long term loan from a mother for this. I regret but you will need to cut the lamb into cubes. This is a labour of love. I got a blister when I performed this operation a few weeks ago. My advice is to do this only at a time when there is a really good long play on the radio to take your mind off the tedium, and use a really sharp knife. Ideally, the tagine will need saffron threads. This is very expensive at home so I always buy some from a supermarket whenever I go abroad. If you haven't got any, substitute turmeric.

	Cook then refrigerate overnight. This will help the meat become unbelievably tender.
Raspberry parfait	Like an ice cream but you will not need an ice cream maker.
Drink	Cotes du Luberon or other regional red
Any other points	Have you put flowers out? Nothing garish. The refined wife of one of my husband's friends has immaculate taste. Angela's life seems to be lived in a palette of creams and beige. And no doubt a legion of cleaners. When she organised *fleurs* for the tables at her son's fabulous *bar mitzvah* (see Chapter 14) they were a discreet sea of cream or white. Incidentally, whilst I like white flowers, I hate lilies because of the stamens which must be snipped off. Everyone knows the pollen stains so, do you agree with me, that this is the hope/expectation when some visitors proffer you a bunch?

Lamb tagine

I actually have a special tagine dish with a conical lid and often wonder why. What on earth am I supposed to do with it when it doesn't appear to be heatproof? I bought it in a market in France probably because the handsome stallholder resembled (in physical appearance that is) my cousin Jonathan. Jonathan is a brilliant and dapper solicitor and it is odd that I can imagine him being good at selling North African tat on a market stall.

Raspberry parfait

The main course was substantial so you really only need a light sweet to finish with. A good parfait perhaps. NB when it comes to the kiddy winks (0-18) I have, after all, decided this is OK for them too – instead of freezing one big log, save petit filous yoghurt pots, buy some ice lolly sticks (obtainable in packets of 50/100) from old fashioned hardware stores, and make mini ice creams to rot their toothy pegs.

Menu 3

(How many of these wretched dinner parties are you supposed to be cooking? He had better be making lots of money.)

Serrano ham with mango	Buy the ham from a deli counter and lay out on plates at the last minute with slices of mango. Mango is messy so prepare your slices earlier in the day. Drizzle with balsamic vinegar.
Lamb shanks with braised lettuce and saffron mashed potato	**Vampire rating 3** Please be careful if you mash the potatoes with the saffron over a wooden work surface. Like pollen from lilies, beetroot and turmeric, saffron stains. If the two of you were eating alone we would suggest you whisked the potato with an electric whisk for a lighter texture but the result is not worth your time at a formal party when your priority should be on ensuring that everything is going smoothly. Just put masses of butter in, what's not to like?
Honeycomb ice cream	Good enough to make it again isn't it?
Drink	Any claret.

Serrano Ham with mango and a peach sauce

We suggest Serrano rather than Parma* because it has a sweet succulent flavour. Untrue, I am not sure I could tell them apart, but everyone does Parma ham with melon and we are trying to be a bit more inventive. It will look as though you have a genuine reason for going Spanish.

Menu 4

Why didn't he tell you they were veggies until now? It serves him right if you have to make a plum bottling savoury pie** – He will be so grateful you can produce something at short notice for one of the partners in his office (whose apartment he wants to borrow in St Tropez) that I guarantee he will overlook your transgression.

*Apologies to Parma. It is a jewel of a city in the Po valley and great for a short trip. Most people go to nearby Bologna, which is nice, but touristy, so forget this and zip down the road to Parma. As you approach it you will see lorries transporting pigs and you know they are on a one way trip. The city is one giant food emporium. Incomparable Parma ham and Parmesan cheese. Heaven. The merchants must have made a mint which explains why the architecture is spectacular. A good venue for a grand gesture.

**I would urge you to keep what I call a *'just in case'* dish in the freezer for this sort of eventuality. If you have unexpected visitors or guests who overstay their welcome and your fridge is empty, it is a life saver to be able to pull a culinary rabbit out of the hat. I tend to have a *pissaladiere* in reserve. This is a wonderful tart filled with a layer of onion cooked with rosemary and then a layer of tomato sauce. On the top is a criss-cross effect made from anchovies and black olives. Put on the anchovies when reheating in case you are faced with strict veggies.

Perfect asparagus	
Polenta with mushrooms	**Vampire rating 3**
Onion tart with a salad of cos lettuce, avocado pear and red pepper with balsamic vinegar dressing	
Tiramisu	
Drink	Sarah and I disagree about booze. I would say stick to champagne throughout. She thinks this could get a bit repetitive and would switch to white wine for the main course. How, *how* can champagne be repetitive Sarah? No bubbles, no fun, I say!

Perfect asparagus /polenta with mushrooms

Both asparagus and mushrooms can be delectable but *only* if they are really fresh. I have found adequate asparagus from a supermarket, but rarely sensational mushrooms. I am reinforced in this view having just eaten a bowl of mushroom soup with mushrooms bought from an old fashioned fruiterer in a local village. CookSmart dictates that if you can't lay your hands on top quality mushrooms skip to the '*just in case*' dish in the freezer.

Tiramisu

Yum, yum, yum. I make an *oeuf* free creation based on a newspaper cutting. I call it tiramisu but Italian mamas might faint if they knew that this dessert was being made without real sponge or raw eggs. For the base I use ye olde sponge fingers dunked in sweetened coffee and whatever strong alcohol is handy. As you know, I have foresworn raw eggs.

All you need is marscapone and sugar, whisked double cream and melted white chocolate and dark chocolate on top. Because the ingredients are all totally, but totally wonderful, it really will not matter if you tinker with the quantities. You could add coffee liqueur to the base – I never have it in the house. Or dark chocolate instead of milk. Chocolate buttons instead of sprinkles. This is about the most foolproof dessert you could throw at your guests.

SCORE

1. *Commitment*	8	He is impressed.
2. *Romance*	0	You are both too tired.
3. *Fun*	6	You are impressed with yourself. This was a triumph.

PS A former colleague of mine once said in jest, I think, that the definition of a secret was something you tell to one person at a time. But you will not be mentioning the fact that the partner's wife disclosed to you in confidence that her husband was having an affair with one of the girls in the MOD's office. This sort of thing is probably common knowledge anyway but it would be wise not to pass on office tittle tattle.

I am good at keeping secrets. Sarah is dreadful.

chapter 14

Off-duty drinks parties

Christmas is coming, the geese are getting fat.
Anonymous

Inspiration

Elizabeth Taylor of course - a legendary beauty who got her man (eight husbands I think, including Richard Burton – twice). Worth renting *Cat on a Hot Tin Roof to* check out her wardrobe particularly the stunning short white cocktail dress. Note too the importance of killer heels.

'Tis the season of goodwill. And this year it will be kick-started with a small gathering of close friends at the beginning of December.

The MOD says he has invited fourteen select people for early evening drinks and nibbles after work. This means anything between 21 and 45 people since he is bound not to have counted his bridge partner, Marcus and wife, Amelie, the neighbours (both sides), the parents and his sister and the entire rugby club. Surely every family has an 'Arnold' - a generic name for that cousin/god parent/uncle who has not made an appearance at 'family functions' for two years. He 'works late'/is 'still in Geneva' or, better still, is 'supervising homework'. Am I a cynic or is this a euphemism for going down the pub or watching telly? Nor do we have to worry about Joshie (single best friend) and Charlie (the ex). They may say they are coming, but mark my words, they are still *broigus* (sic having a feud) with you and will get stuck at work. Hurray!

Survive this party and you are set for Christmas *chez les parents* and maybe a special little package under the tree.

How many really brilliant parties have you been to? Shall we dissect these events and see what turns an affair like this into a damp squib?

- an empty room
- crap '80's music
- warm white wine in paper cups
- supermarket canapés
- hunger
- no loo paper in the cloakroom
- the 'Ambassador's choice' of chocolate – like marmite – you either love or hate them
- your coat getting trampled on.

When I was unattached I would classify parties by 'the talent'. One event stood out. I wore a *very* short silver shift 'man magnet' dress* and blue high heels and was invited out by several guests, one of whom asked if men always fell in love with me.** I was oblivious to

*/** I have found unfortunately that man magnet/results dresses attract interest from men who tend to blurt out extravagantly insincere compliments when they make your acquaintance. Other examples in a similar vein are '*Will you take me to the Caribbean?*', '*you have film star legs*' and '*I find you irredeemably attractive*'. The only redeeming feature about the last was that this was not said as an opening gambit. It was nevertheless meaningless verbal garbage. I would say wear something more demure (I mean not tarty - but glamorous) if you want a serious relationship, but this is a conclusion you need to reach.

the catering arrangements but I have a vague feeling it was just a crisps and white wine job.

When you are no longer scouring the room for a mate, you begin to pay more attention to props such as good food and drink. Flirting with other men can get you into hot water so you need something more tangible to make an evening bearable.

Nowadays, I look forward to an annual summer drinks party given by a bachelor friend of Stephen's, Horatio. He is at the Bar and is probably emulating a chambers' bash since these tend to be catered impressively. Whilst his *soirées* are predictable in that there will inevitably be wall-to-wall champagne (I ain't complaining), there is enough of a variety of up-market canapés to maintain interest and the event is always packed – so if you tire of talking to someone you are unlikely to run into them again in the crush.

Certainly, the food you serve will show what you think of your guests. The husband of one couple we know is a business 'leader' (his wife told me that they had even breakfasted with Tony Blair at No.10). When Joel first reached the dizzy corporate heights we attended a sensationally chic party at their cream-carpeted house - or should I say villa? Even the waiters wore uniforms that I swear were designed by Jasper Conran. Nibbles were first rate. I have since borrowed the idea of serving small shot glasses with chilled borsht – beetroot soup.

Fast forward four years and another of their do's. This was plainly for 'D' listers (that's us) and/or business 'losers' (yup) since this time the young sons were manning the trays. Instead of fancy finger food, it was inferior Chinese take away. Annoyingly, the dry cleaners were unable to remove a brown grease stain on my new red dress dripped from some liquidy sauce.

Nowt so queer as folk. On another occasion we trekked a hundred or so miles for a birthday party. I can only guess that the hosts were trying to appear bohemian and arty. The birthday girl and her husband, Jack and Jill (well – why not? They are perfectly good

171

names) *are* bohemian and arty. Usually, I find them hugely
entertaining and we get a decent meal. That time, it was three hours
for the round trip to be greeted with little more than wine and bowls
of boiled eggs, bread and cheese. I have had more generous fare at
impoverished student parties. We did not wait to see if there would
be any other party food; hunger led to our making our excuses and
heading for the chip shop. Fortunately, we chanced upon an
excellent chippie and, as a one-off treat, Stephen actually let me eat
in his precious car.

People

For a party that goes with a swing you must fill the room. There is
no magic number; it is literally a question of how much space you
have. So, size up the sitting room and calculate the minimum number
of bodies you need. Then, invite a few 'B list' friends to come too. No
need to tell the MOD – he will be glad you did this on the day.

Next, manoeuvre matters so that the event takes place on a Friday
(you will have to take the day off work to get things ready) or
preferably, Saturday. If it goes ahead on a week day you *will* end up
with half the guests you expect.

For our last party, we made the mistake of holding it on a Thursday.
It went off okay but there were quite a few last minute drop-outs.
Two lawyers claimed that meetings with clients overran, two
bankers were in New York, one businessman was stranded at a fog
bound airport and his heavily pregnant wife did not feel like coming
on her own, the female half of the couple who enjoyed her private
jet was an unexplained no show, perhaps it was the absence of a
nearby helipad, and an *uber* mother cried off *by e-mail* at the
eleventh hour because she had to ferry her daughter, a reservist in
an inter school gymnastic competition, to the other side of town.
She was so sorry they *both* couldn't make it. She added that
Thursdays are always difficult for her husband. Quite sensibly,
married women don't like their good looking partners to go to
shindigs without them. They know about women like Charlie.

I have a freezer full of surplus mushroom *vol au vents* if you are interested.

Party food

Well executed clichéd '70's food is actually what people want unless you can afford the very best outside catering. The two of us have been to many catered parties with soggy low grade *canapés* that have no doubt cost a fortune. Yours won't and they will be tasty.

1. *Little cocktail sausages basted in honey and wholegrain mustard*	Remember to have a saucer or bowl for guests to put their cocktail sticks in. No one wants to see saliva covered sticks propped up on the side of the serving dish. YUK, YUK, YUK! Plus upmarket wipes or cocktail napkins and visible attractive waste paper bins.
2. *Small duck pancakes filled with strips of cooked duck breast, plum sauce and cucumber matchsticks*	It is no good buying in pancakes. These MUST be home made. Add a couple of tablespoons of cognac to the mix to give them extra oomph. Cook the duck the day before the party but do not cut up the meat until the next day. Seal it with cooking juices. Don't overdo the sauce or you'll have gooey brown drips on your carpet. Were you making these for four I would serve them warm but you will not want to be doing this sort of last minute preparation in your LBD so you will be eating them at room temperature.
3. *Your home made potato pancakes with smoked salmon*	

4. *Good ol'fashioned pineapple with cheese on sticks. Or if you can't go that retro – mango and manchego.*	Better still, find small or medium wooden skewers. I eventually tracked some down in a kitchen shop and hoovered up a lifetime's supply. A good tip when disposing of skewers/cocktail sticks is to put them in empty soft drinks bottles or boxes so that the Dish and refuse collectors don't get skewered by sharp sticks when lifting the rubbish bags. We are considerate!
5. *Asparagus wraps*	You are familiar with these by now. Use parma ham and/or smoked salmon.
6. *Mini pizzas*	Hey - Why not get the kids to make these for you on one of their visits? I like the idea of putting them to work. I wonder if they can do anything else useful too?
7. *Mini quiches*	Think you can handle pastry? Of course. Two tips: Pancetta is easier to work with than bacon if you were going to do quiche lorraine and whisking egg with *crème fraiche* makes a good basic flan filling. Just add cheese, tomato, cooked veg such as leek and the cooked meat.
8. *Aunt Jessica's mince pies*	Her secret for superlative mince is to use fresh cranberries and orange juice.
9. *Mini ice creams*	Collect petit filou pots and fill them with honeycomb ice cream mixture and shove in a wooden lolly stick. Or, if you cant be bothered, buy some mini ices but they tend to be quite pricey.
10. *Plenty of crisps, nuts and twiglets*	
Drink	Mulled wine.
Music	Up to date party mixes or perhaps a theme.

> You may need more than one since Latino
> music can get a bit samey after half an hour.
> The idea of having several contrasting
> moods is not a bad one.

2. Duck pancakes

The first unveiling of this exquisite delicacy. If you make and freeze
the pancakes a couple of weeks earlier then all you have to do is
defrost, then reheat them in the oven, covered with foil. Remove
from the oven and fill as you would a pancake at your local Chinese.

PS I am completing this chapter way after midnight having just
returned from Angela and Sheldon's spectacular *bar mitzvah* party
at a fancy central London hotel. Lest mine hosts are reading this,
please do not think I am being critical. It was fabulous – I hope I did
not disrupt your table plan by moving around the table slightly – it
was to get away from the table leg, not the pillar, and I look forward
to the *bar mitzvah* boy's sister's *bat mitzvah* at the same venue.

NB if you are having a sit-down event it is sensible to position men
by table legs since female guests, other than exhibitionists, may be
reluctant to hike a straight skirted long dress to thigh level in order
to sit down.

Why do I mention the do though? Well, we sampled lots of *canapés*
– for research purposes you understand – and agreed that my duck
pancakes were better than the duck spring rolls we ate tonight. Yes,
yes, yes!

By the bye, I particularly loved the pink champagne for the reception
and the diamond shaped smoked salmon and cream cheese *canapés*.
What's more, having recommended that *you* make sushi for the
'step children' I was delighted to see a sushi bar which really
attracted the youngsters.

This no-expense-spared *soirée* also featured *three* bands. If you are

175

operating to a more modest budget I happen to know *one* brilliant and beguiling musician – who can turn his hands to three different kinds of music. Need his number?

7. Mini quiches
To make life easy, buy a mini muffin tray and some ordinary fairy cake cases. Line the tray with the cases. Roll out the pastry and, using a round cutter, stamp circles of pastry to fit the inside of the cases. Do not be tempted to choose the smallest sized cutter since you will find that you need as much pastry for each individual *canapé* as you would for a normal fairy cake sized hole in a fairy cake tray. Sarah's surprised that you can do pastry in paper cake cases but you can. It's not as fiddly as it sounds.

I cook the pastry at 180 for approx 5 mins so that it retains its shape. Lauren, the restaurateur friend I have mentioned to you previously (who is a superb cook), says she does not pre-bake the shell, but there we are. I know my method works. Make up your own mind whether to follow the advice of a haphazard amateur who has got you this far, or a professional whose *canapés* are an unknown quantity. You are between a rock and a hard place!

8. Home made mince pies
I make a couple of boxes of mince pies for my husband's office every year and everyone always raves about them. Yes, my better half is the guvnor. But, if they hated them they would tell his PA, who is a friend of mine and I would hope she would tell me.

Perfect party beverages

This really is a difficult one. For a summer party we would have said champagne is easy. You can't beat bubbles to get everyone into the mood. Sangria is delectable too (neither of us are snobs – about drink anyway) but to some it will not have unfortunately shrugged off its white stiletto connotations.

Sarah has a Spanish friend who pronounces it SanGREE-ya , and she should know, so that's the way she always announces it at a party, with a flourish and a fabulous earthy accent.

For a wintry gathering, table wine is a little dull and difficult to serve at the right temperature. How about mulled wine? It is festive, slightly different and shows an extra level of preparation. But it has to be top notch. I have a recipe from Nancy, a friend of Hermione's, which bears a manuscript note saying it was made for a Guy Fawkes party in 1965.

Nance helpfully says you can make the syrup in advance. Use a funnel to decant it into bottles (start to collect some washed empty bottles a few weeks before your party if you do not have those large jars for making jam/pickles) so it can be added to the red wine on the evening.

You don't want to be caught like a friend of Sarah's with 8 zillion 2-litre plastic bottles of industrial cheapo mulled wine stacked on the kitchen table when you're trying to give the impression you've slaved over it yourself from an old family recipe!

The wine needs to be served warm but not hot. You may wish to use tumblers or mugs– ask your mother if it's an old wives' tale that you should prop up a spoon in a glass to prevent it from cracking. And watch your cream carpets! Peter's banned any dark liquids from any room which doesn't have wooden floors in their house. He is a right old woman about it, but he does have immaculate carpets.

Achievement and expectations – Aunt Jessica comes to stay

The preparations for the party are going well, the kitchen is a hive of activity, exuding the gorgeous aromas from a miscellany of bubbling pots. There is only one hitch. Unless Aunt Jessica has moved in, even the Dish might begin to wonder where all the pastry and pancakes have come from.

While you are getting him to sample his second or third mulled wine it is time to test his sense of humour and to slip into the conversation that Dear Auntie has met with a terrible accident, but not before imparting to you her 95 years of cooking skills. You get the drift. The MOD needs to be told that Guess Who made the mince pies? It will come as a delightful surprise to you at this stage that, he will be so consumed with admiration for your cuisine and that you are so low maintenance, that we can lay to rest his fear of the Plum Bottler for good.

SCORE

1. *Commitment*   9   You were perfect hosts

2. *Romance*   5   It depends how much *vin chaud* he has drunk.

3. *Fun*   7   It was a lot of work but you were a party girl.

chapter 15
Grand gestures and little gems
Gifts which hit the target and those which miss the mark

"What really flatters a man is that you think him worth flattering"
George Bernard Shaw(1856-1950) Irish playwright

Inspiration

For this we ask you to put on your thinking cap and try and recall which of your girlfriends has spent an inordinate amount of money as an investment on their boyfriends to good effect.

Grand gestures

Not wishing to go over old ground we would simply remind you that a man will take a gift at face value. A woman will analyse what it is, why it was given and try and work out how much it cost. In contrast, the degree of pleasure a man derives from a present is directly proportional to it's magnitude. This is the principle underpinning the grand gesture. It's success lies in the fact that men have big egos; as a corollary an apparently spontaneous, generous and exciting gesture will be tremendously flattering.

Before you rush off and book the Dish a weekend at the *luxe* Parisian hotel (I am guessing) *Le Crillon* – wait one second. There is a difference between a grand gesture and a romantic one. The latter, like my doomed heart-shaped pizza, will have the opposite effect. So by all means treat the chap to a trip somewhere fun – Barcelona, Berlin, New York, Milan, Le Touquet etc but avoid destinations with primarily romantic associations such as Paris or Rome. Let him whisk you off there!

But why not romantic? We are back to the old pressure issue. You need to lead your fellow to water but he must drink himself.

Grand gestures to make
Weekends away
How about a city break somewhere he has not been to before? Like Madrid, Lyons, St Petersburg. Limit air travel to a maximum of six hours and definitely avoid overnight flights or destinations which spell (a) jet lag on the return and (b) smelly armpits.

A designer suit
Corduroy or velvet perhaps.

A black or oyster faced Jaeger le Coutre, Omega or similar 'once in a lifetime' watch
Undoubtedly handsome. Too smothering though unless you have been dating for at least 6 months.

A day's ballooning
Bet this is something he has not done. Check the safety record. I am not sure I would pay for someone I cared for to have flying lessons.

A bottle of Dom Perignon or Krug
A special treat to share. Being champers this would generally be on

the forbidden list but it is so special I think he will appreciate this. Do not bring two crystal glasses, in fact, to make it more humorous serve in paper cups in bed, of course.

Grand gestures not to make

1. A love child

This form of 'gift' must be approached with extreme caution and is best avoided please. The term 'a love child' and the phrase 'being required to have a paternity test' often go hand in hand, so we are not entirely certain we understand what a love child means. Devotion cannot always be on a man's mind in *flagrante delecto* and knowingly setting about to become pregnant without sharing your plans with your partner is an underhand strategy incompatible with the spirit of grand gestures which should aim to confer an uncomplicated message of adoration.

It is self evident that pregnancy *on its own* will not necessarily result in a man doing 'the decent thing'. However, a little one on its way combined with a grand gesture might mean you stand a better chance of commitment.

2. A luxurious train journey

This will be considered romantic *pants*. You might be thinking a long train journey together is romantic. He will be glued to *The Economist* wishing you had flown.

3. Expensive ski hols

Weekends away are one thing but this means Friday to Sunday. And, unless you can think of a resort which is comfortably within reach of an international airport, you risk spending a large chunk of your short break on a transfer bus waiting for some annoying passengers to embark after the loo stops.

For anything longer than a weekend and however fab you may look in your all white ski ensemble, the MOD *must* be the one to treat you. No harm in familiarising yourself with some charming hotels in the main ski resorts if you think that an invitation to hit the *piste* is on the cards. I can recommend *La Pomme de Pain* in Courcheval and *Hotel Alex* in Zermatt.

Little gems

These are going to be useful now and then. We are simply going to list a few of these thoughtful frivolous things you can do or buy to win you extra brownie points from time to time.

Gestures to make

For weekends away produce one of those third sized bottles of champagne
Great for après-ski.

Take him out for a fun meal
As a thank you perhaps. I took Stephen to the quaint White Tower restaurant after I got a new job. I can't recall what part he played in that process.

You should aim for somewhere with excellent food, verve and imagination rather than a place which is just popular for five minutes. Avoid anything too expensive. How about a good Indian or Italian? Avoid chains and try and find a family-run place.

Try an Indian restaurant near Brick Lane rather than your local curry house.

A country pub with tried and tested food in a picturesque setting. Especially "with rooms". Men love staggering upstairs to sleep it off, then brekky in the morning.

Picnic on the beach at Le Touquet or Southend.

Buy a funky shirt
He will like being thought of as cutting edge.

How about an initialised cufflink box?
I gave a silver one to Stephen on the first birthday after we met. Funnily enough since we have got married presents have gone downhill a bit. I don't remember what I gave him for his last one. I am sure it was very sweet.

A trouser press?
Don't laugh! The closest I have come to divorce was when I asked a builder to dump Stephen's old one on the skip. It turned out to have been a present from his ex. My mother recognised the danger and bought him a replacement PDQ.

A set of decent waterproofs for golf
It shows you have an interest in his game!

A Noel Cowardesque dressing gown
You have to get him out of towelling. White waffle cloth is good too.

A CD for his car
Nothing romantic. Head banging heavy metal is best.

Tickets for a Big Match
You will need some help here as to which one.

Tickets for the Rolling Stones
You will enjoy this too.

Speedy Boarding
For a couple of pounds you can purchase the right to priority boarding on the budget airlines. He may be embarrassed about going 'sub-cattle' in the first place but this at least will mean that you do not have to queue with everyone. Well, not queue exactly since the last time I went on this type of airline it was more of a rugby scrum than an orderly queue.

An unusual cinema trip
I saw *'Casino Royale'* the first time (yes, I have a crush on Daniel)

at the Everyman in Hampstead. Wowie. I have not been to the flicks like this before. There are similar cinemas in other towns. They have armchairs and settees for two which you can pre-book and little illuminated tables for drinks. The bar sells champagne and truffles. A luxurious gesture.

Books and talks at bookshops by leading authors
Something intellectual – any 19ᵗʰ century Russian novel will make you look well-read.

Anything monogrammed
Brief cases, shirts but never handkerchiefs. Who wants to launder these?

An overnight case/suit hanging bag
If he travels frequently he may think of you when he is away.

Now for the ones to steer clear of

Gestures to avoid
Boxer shorts
Too tacky. Every other girlfriend has given him a set with the words 'HOT STUFF!' or 'BIG BOY' on the front.

Cookwear
He will be frightened.

Hip flasks
A bit old fashioned.

Tickets for Take That
Keep these for your girlfriends.

Books on gardening, cricket or meditation
Mogadon.

An Arsenal season ticket
You need to accompany him for the gift to have a full impact. He

will not take you more than once.

Knitwear
Leave that to Nan. They will probably have been on sale at John Lewis and still have the price tag on. Apologies to one of my favourite shops, I am not sure they have sales. Aren't they called 'seasonal reductions'?

After shave, smellies, pens and ties
Boring and done to death by your predecessors and his siblings. Gimmicky gifts like pen torches for reading maps, mini fans, hot water bottle covers etc This is the sort of gift his mother would buy him at Christmas when she has run out of ideas for anything he actually might want or find useful.

Sale items
Do not bestow a gift of anything bought in a sale. If he takes it back to the shop he will think less of you when he finds out you bought him this unwanted item because it was cheap. It would be a false economy that could cost you dear.

Recycled gifts
Don't pretend you don't know what I am referring to. *Everyone* has a present drawer with strange pressies which we are just waiting to palm off onto someone else. The MOD will know you do this. Especially don't do it, as a friend of Sarah's did, without noticing that it had been inscribed to HER before she passed it on to Sarah.

Lurking in my cupboard I still have left:

* a toy climbing cat that sticks to an outside wall
* a weird kind of gymnastic ball – could be a sex toy?
* a poker set
* a cheap boxed set of gardening gloves and pruners
* a 24 piece cutlery set.

Any takers?

chapter 16

Triumph
Announcing the alliance (engagement) to the family at dinner

"Diamonds are a girl's best friend"
Leo Robin (1900-1984) American composer and lyricist

Congratulations! *Mazel tov!* Etc etc.

Inspiration

YOU! So what if he did not get down on bended knee in a conservatory with a string ensemble and you wearing a frilly cream frock. It is people, not places which matter. There was a line in John Osborne's *Look Back in Anger* – it went something like this – '*he made sitting next to him on the top deck of a bus feel like you were setting out on a journey with Ulysess.*' Ever felt like that?

Count yourself fortunate to have had a proposal – it was only a couple of hours before our two families met that I extracted some sort of mumbled commitment from Stephen. Needless to say I paid him back by insisting upon a decent rock. For those of you who know as little as I did about diamonds, it is not all about size. Stones are graded according to quality; good ones sparkle in the light. However, even if you need an electron microscope to see the stone, the litmus test is whether gazing at it in the office cheers you up when you are bored.

Let's get back to business. There's many a slip between cup and lip. Part of the courting ritual which must be endured is the meeting of the parents. It is unlikely that they will have anything in common and the best you can hope for is that they tolerate each other. An enjoyable meal could help foster an *entente cordiale*.

Make this seminal meeting your *pièce de resistance*.

Now that you are an ENGAGED WOMAN you qualify for serving a family roast. However, tread warily. Your 'mum-in-law' should preserve her monopoly on beef, lamb and chicken - you must not upstage her before the wedding. The MOD knows that you are in a different league by now. The obvious choice is a fabulous duck *à l'orange*.

NB. Since you propose to cook duck for the main course and chicken liver *parfait* for *canapés* you had better find out if the MOD's father suffers from gout. You hadn't thought of this, had you? This is exactly why you still need me. People suffering from gout are not supposed to eat duck or liver. I have given you an alternative main course.

We do not wish to be presumptuous but, since this is a 'once in a lifetime' occasion (ok – he's been married four times before, but hope springs eternal), it is appropriate to offer a tray of *canapés* with champagne when you receive the inevitable toast before dinner.

We *know* that it will come as a bit of a shock to you that it does not cross your mind for even a second to buy in some appetisers. This is firstly because, although this cooking business started out as a bit of fun, a game of sorts, somewhere *en route* you have imperceptibly metamorphosed into the confident hostess with high standards and an eye for detail that you were trying to emulate. What's more, you actually care for the MOD and bask in his evident admiration of your culinary abilities. Significantly, this means that you could make your own delectable chicken liver parfait.

Menu

Canapés *of toasted squares with home made chicken liver* parfait *and onion marmalade*	**Vampire rating 2** Enhance the flavour of the pâté with Cognac.
Marinated cod and halibut served on a bed of rocket and spinach leaves	The idea of this starter is that it is sophisticated and not too filling and it can be made in advance.
Duck à l'orange *with* potatoes *dauphinoise and* petits pois/*tomato flavoured chicken casserole with rice and sugar snap peas*	**Vampire rating 2 each dish** If you have to make the chicken dish cook this the day before. Give it body with fried onion and garlic.
Rice pudding with rum flavoured raisins	I think you realise I am joking here. Remember what I have said about hot desserts. This is not a meal to fluff. Serve a cold delight for 'afters'. A chocolate tart would be perfect.
Drink	Champagne, of course. Tattinger is my preference.

the dish

Music	I think not.
Dress	Be yourself.
Any other points?	Best check what your mother is planning to wear.

Achievement and expectations

Mission accomplished I think you would say!

SCORE

1. *Commitment*	10	You have got the ring.
2. *Romance*	10	*Magnifique!*
3. *Fun*	10	This was your triumph.

A full house.

chapter 17

Top tips on how to be CookSmart

"She was no prisoner, and I want to make that clear at the outset"
The Killjoy by Anne Fine (1947-)
British children's author

Now that we have reached the end of this culinary expedition let's see if you have been paying attention. We set out below the principal tenets of our 'philosophy' of CookSmart. We think you will find them considerably more useful than Descartes!

1. Buy the best and freshest ingredients

Be bold. Make a conscious decision to abandon a recipe if you are unable to find good enough ingredients. Unripe tomatoes are underpowered. Full stop.

Let's say something about delis. If you have a good one, patronise it. Regrettably, most of the ones I have tried have struck me as being overpriced and poncey. We would prefer to get delicious salami from the nice Turkish man at the market.

2. You should buy in

We have agreed, haven't we, that even now you can be a Plum Bottler, there are certain things that really ought to be bought in, because they are more trouble than they are worth to make.

These items are bread (I know it is obvious but some people still make it), pastries and fruit tarts, soups, baked beans, ice cream and yoghurt. Going back to bread, if you *have* been given a breadmaker, like Sarah, it is simplicity itself to bung some ingredients in, and it can be really nice with soup for a dinner party. Fills the house with lovely smells too.

We also do not see why you could not buy good *canapés* from say a local restaurant which does not normally do take-aways. You may find that some of them have catering services for parties. I know my limitations. Because I have not got a deep fat fryer I would not attempt to fry fish or chips. But, I would not hesitate to ask our lovely local Italian restaurant *Mezzaluna* to rustle up 50 *goujons* for me if I needed them. You would be surprised how accommodating chefs will be.

3. Take-away food

However good a cook you are, sometimes the Dish will have a desperate craving for curry! And so might you. Yield to it. Do some research and find out which local restaurants do the best take-away curry, Chinese and fish and chips. For the record, in my neighbourhood, I recommend the Shah Bhag in Hampstead Village, Weng Wah in Belsize Park and the Nautilus in West Hampstead. Yum yum.

Aimée, a local pal, who is more organised that I could ever be, proudly showed me a folder she keeps in her kitchen with pristine take-away menus in individual clear plastic wallets. Honestly, I do keep my bank statements in coherent date order, but I confess that other documentation is stored in an alphabetically divided briefcase using my personal filing system which baffles Stephen. *I* know what I am doing.

4. Embrace big flavours

You have probably noticed that just about every savoury dish contains garlic in abundance. We like strong peasant fare. You can imagine recipes being handed down the generations from mother to daughter.

This fondness for robustness applies equally to wine, herbs and spices. Just about any meat will gain extra zest if marinated overnight. The process also tenderises the meat. For lamb cutlets for example, it takes a few seconds to prepare a simple marinade using liberal quantities of olive oil, garlic, lemon juice and grated lemon rind. Throw in whatever fresh herbs you have to hand too.

A little trick I learned from a wonderful Italian restaurant tucked away in a back street of Islington, *Pizza Oregano*, is to mince garlic and mix it with oil. This can be added at the last minute to a bolognaise sauce. This technique could be used for just about any casserole or pasta sauce to lend a bit of rocket fuel.

5. Adopt a *laissez faire* CookSmart approach to quantities

We hope you have acquired the confidence to follow your instincts, to CookSmart.

The essence of this approach is to be able to judge for yourself how much to use of key ingredients to suit your palate and the occasion.

Hence, we would tone down the garlic and herbs for a cottage pie destined for the prospective parents-in-law. But, were we preparing the same meal for two we might well try out the garlic infused oil.

It is imperative that you feel free to experiment by adjusting one ingredient or another.

6. Pre-prepared is good

There is a heavy accent on cooking in advance. This has two advantages. Firstly, there is the practical benefit that it gives you the leisure and freedom both to plan ahead and to concentrate on being a hostess during the event, instead of having to hover over the cooker. Secondly, the end product of many a creation is infinitely tastier if it can rest for several hours.

Finally, we would reiterate that it is a good idea to keep a range of 'just in case' dishes in your freezer as stand bys.

7. The drinks cabinet

Spirits
- You will need a full bottle of the following: Premium gin, preferably Tanqueray or Plymouth. According to my husband these are cocktail strength at 47.5% alcohol. It probably explains why he is half cut by 8.30pm.
- Genuine Russian vodka such as Stolichnya.
- Martini extra dry.
- An expensive Cognac plus a cheaper one for cooking.
- Malt whisky.

Table wine
The meals in this book have all had a wine chosen for them but there will be a frequent, dare I say, constant, requirement for glasses of wine without food. For this we would find a decent local offie.

Oddbins is pretty good. Ask them to recommend a Macon and sample a few as you will be drinking this one yourself. This is a Chardonnay from the white Burgundy region. You should not expect to pay more than £6-7 a bottle.

For red, a good all rounder is the *Crozes Hermitages* area. According to the man of the family who slurps this, it is the Syrah grape and it goes as well with gutsy food or on its own. Similar pricing should apply.

Keep a case of each on hand. You will get a discount for buying in bulk, and believe me you will drink it! Now, both our husbands are wine buffs, and we are happy to just drink it. But men find it attractive in a woman that she is able to choose a half drinkable bottle in a restaurant, or pick one out from the supermarket/offie unaided. So just follow out tips above, to fulfil this requirement.

Beer
His brand – have plenty of it.

For you, Italian lager.

8. Equipment

You will have already seen the usefulness of my treasured *bain marie*. The other essential is a dishwasher. Even if you have a small kitchen the mini ones are better than nothing.

Conclusion

Well, our protégée, you have navigated your way from a can't-boil-an-egg ditz to a confident, assured society hostess! You've won friends and influenced people. You've got the Dish to fall in love with you: your curves and your quiches, your laughter and your lemon tart, your jokes and your jellies, as it were. And you've won over his mother, more to the point. We wish you every success in the kitchen, dining room, bedroom, at the altar (chuppa etc) and beyond (not necessarily in that order).

Bon appetit!